From Venus to Victoria

a history of Fortfield Terrace and Sidmouth
1790 - 1901

to Peter and Jill
from the author and resident of No. 8

PETER FUNG

Peter Fung
2012

ortfield
publishing

SIDMOUTH 2012

Cover and title page illustration from Stereoview of Fortfield Terrace by Francis Bedford 1868

First published in the United Kingdom in 2012

A CIP catalogue record for this book is available from the British Library.

Paperback ISBN 978-0-9570638-0-8

Designed and published by
Fortfield Publishing
8 Fortfield Terrace
SIDMOUTH
Devon
EX10 8NT
ffpsidmouth@btinternet.com

Printed and bound by
Westprint
Clyst Court
Blackmore Road
Hill Barton Business Park
Clyst St Mary,
EXETER
EX5 1SA

FROM VENUS TO VICTORIA

TABLE OF CONTENTS

ACKNOWLEDGEMENTS

I am grateful to all who have provided information and given permission for images to be used in this book.

Specific sources are cited throughout the text and listed in the reference section at the end of the book. Images are fully attributed in the list of illustrations. I have made every attempt to obtain relevant copyright permissions, but if there are any omissions, these will be corrected in subsequent editions.

I would like to thank the following for the use of their resources and facilities:
Bristol Record Office
Devon Record Office
Shropshire Record Office
Sidmouth Library
West Country Studies Library, Exeter
and especially Maureen Church and other staff at Sidmouth Museum for their help and access to the collection.

Thanks also to the Sid Vale Association for their encouragement of this project, to Julia Creeke for her suggestions and sharing of her wide knowledge of the history of Sidmouth, and to Nigel Hyman for historical insights into King George III.

I am grateful to my wife, Dilly, and to Rhiannon Hodson and Jonathan Walker for their helpful comments on the final text.

Finally, thanks to friends, family and fellow-residents of Fortfield Terrace, and to Dilly, who share with me a deep appreciation of being part of the history of our beautiful town and Terrace.

FOREWORD

Sidmouth is a town of many pleasant sights and memories. One of these is a Georgian terrace that looks down across the cricket ground and croquet lawns towards the sea. Fortfield Terrace has featured in all of the guide books written about Sidmouth, spanning the last two centuries.

In 1836 Theodore Mogridge, local doctor and once resident of Fortfield Terrace, wrote in his *Descriptive Sketch of Sidmouth,* 'Opposite is a large field, called Fort Field…on which is a fine open terrace, lined with a row of excellent houses, commanding a varied and extensive prospect.'[1]

Over a century later, Sir John Betjeman wrote, 'I doubt if anywhere on the south coast there is a prettier Georgian stucco crescent than Fortfield Terrace which overlooks the cricket ground'.[2] In 1962, before he became Poet Laureate, he wrote *Still Sidmouth,* to accompany a television documentary about the town. In the poem he refers to the Terrace:

> *See when the sun is at its noon-day height,*
> *Regency ironwork, elegant and light,*
> *It stands out grim against the stucco's white.*
> *Broad crescents basking in the summer sun,*
> *A sense of sea and holidays begun,*
> *Leisure to live and breathe and smell and look,*
> *Unfold for me this seaside history book.*
>
> *…Then to watch cricket on the fairest ground,*
> *That ring which exists all England round,*
> *And although cricket bores me, here I find*
> *The pleasant scenery, I ease my mind.*
> *Sun-smitten terrace, sound of ball on bat,*
> *And in the quiet the sudden cry "How's that!"*
> *The keen sea air so keeps my brain awake,*
> *That even I can some interest take.*[3]

The Terrace has not only inspired travel writers and poets, but also architects. Following the Second World War, the architect, Frederick Gibberd, was involved in the planning of Harlow, in Essex. He created an impressive crescent of terraced houses - 'New town houses for New Town residents' - which he says was inspired by 'Fortfield Terrace, an elegant early 19th-century development at Sidmouth'.[4]

Fortfield Terrace is a Grade II* Listed curved Georgian Terrace – had it been completed it would have been a crescent. Some of the houses are now owned as single homes, and some are divided into apartments, inhabited by long-term residents, shorter-term tenants or holiday makers. No 10 is the home of the Sidmouth Club, a Gentlemen's Club founded in 1890. To the west of the Terrace is the thatched Cricket Pavilion.

The old wood and coal cellars extend under the raised pavement at the front of the Terrace…

…and at the rear of the Terrace are secluded walled gardens.

Today's visitor approaching the Terrace finds that there are two blue plaques, at Nos 1 and 8, outlining details of particular historic interest, concerning aristocrats, royal visitors and poets who have stayed there.[5]

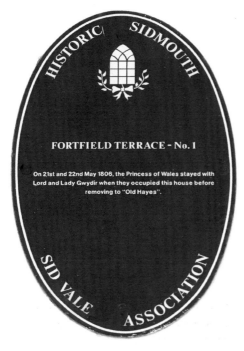

It is these glimpses of a past life, coupled with the frequent enquiries of visitors, local and from afar, that have prompted the writing of this book. As one of those fortunate enough to live in Sidmouth and in Fortfield Terrace, I feel that this is a story that should be told before too much more of its future history is written, and certainly before its past is forgotten. If at times the story seems to ramble and wander in strange directions, it is because, in my opinion, history and life are like that.

PROLOGUE

On 8 June, 2004 an infrequent astronomical event known as 'the transit of Venus' was observable in Sidmouth, as the planet Venus passed between earth and the sun. Shortly after this event, while I was researching this book, I read the following editorial comment in *The Sidmouth Directory and General Advertiser* of 4 December, 1882:

> On Weds next, 6*th* inst., a transit of Venus across the face of the sun will be visible in Sidmouth if the clouds permit. No living man has seen a transit of Venus in England, and no one now alive can ever see one again unless he lives to the year 2004.[1]

These words seem to encapsulate an essential element of human history. As individuals our lives occupy such a short time in the whole scheme of things. Yet as shared human experience, those individual and infinitely valuable short times are part of a greater ongoing long-term picture.

Fortfield Terrace as a building has existed for over two hundred years: during that time many people have been involved with it in one way or another. Some were there for only a few days, others for a large part of their lives. Some were born there, some died there. Some were famous, some obscure. Some were visitors, others local. Some were holiday makers, some worked there. They came from all social backgrounds, from all walks of life. Each had his or her own hopes and aspirations, ambitions and expectations.

They were part of a time of change unprecedented in the world and the nation. It is the coming together of those lives and those times within a framework of bricks and mortar that creates the story of our seaside town and terrace.

CHAPTER ONE
ITALIAN BEGINNINGS

TRANSIT OF VENUS PROHIBITED...

ARTS MINISTER PLACES TEMPORARY EXPORT BAR
ON A ROMAN MARBLE STATUE OF VENUS

Minister of State for the Arts, Estelle Morris, has placed a temporary bar on the export of a Roman marble statue of Venus. It is widely regarded as the most important of the ancient sculptures acquired by William Weddell for Newby Hall in 1765. This will provide a last chance to raise the money to keep the statue in the United Kingdom.

M2 PRESSWIRE 7 August, 2003[1]

In 2002 this statue of Venus was sold at Christie's in London for £7,926,650, a world record price for an antiquity sold at auction. The British Government's attempt to prevent its export failed, and Venus eventually moved to Qatar.

She is known as the *Jenkins Venus*, having been bought by William Weddell in Rome in the spring of 1765 from Thomas Jenkins. Twenty-two years after selling the statue, Thomas Jenkins bought the Sidmouth Manor Estate and shortly after that he commissioned the building of Fortfield Terrace.

It seems fitting that, at a time when Italy was having such an influence on art and architecture in England, the story of Fortfield Terrace should find its origins in Rome.

THE JENKINS VENUS
Newby Hall, Ripon, North Yorkshire

❧ THOMAS JENKINS ❧

Thomas Jenkins was born in Honiton in 1722, the son of William Jenkins. Thomas had an older brother, William, who was Vicar of Upottery. It is likely that their father was also a clergyman. When still a young man, Thomas made his way to Rome to seek his fortune, possibly as the valet to a Grand Tourist. He spent most of the rest of his life there.

In *Sidmouth: A History*[2] he is described as a cleaner and restorer of pictures who dabbled in antiques and then went on to manufacture sham antiques which were palmed off as genuine.

ANNA MARIA JENKINS; THOMAS JENKINS *by Angelica Kauffmann*
National Portrait Gallery, London

This is a rather dismissive assessment of him, probably based mainly on Peter Orlando Hutchinson's representation of him in his *History of Sidmouth,* published in 1880. Hutchinson's views would have been coloured by local speculation which was rife in Sidmouth following the acquisition of the Sidmouth Manor Estate by Thomas Jenkins in 1787. In Hutchinson's words:

> When I was a boy, and when the [Jenkins] *family was more talked of than it has been of later years, I heard many anecdotes related, both of him and his relatives. Besides the cameos and imitation antiques mentioned by Nollekens* [a contemporary British sculptor]*, there seems to have been a belief in Sidmouth that he manufactured figures or statuettes, which, with the other trinkets, were buried near the Coliseum, to be dug up before the eyes of visitors, and sold at high prices. John Ebdon, my late father's carpenter, when alluding one day to the irregular courses into which most of the family were running, said to me – "I tell 'e what it is sir – Them there Jenkinses won't never come to no good, because they got their money by worshiping graven images."* [3]

A different perspective on Jenkins' life can be seen in the description of him by art historians and contemporary society figures as a banker and wealthy art dealer who lived in Rome, and was engaged in securing commissions for the British artists residing there and in buying works of art for noblemen on the Grand Tour. Among many famous sculptures, he acquired Bernini's *Neptune and Triton*, now in the Victoria and Albert Museum, for Joshua Reynolds. He was certainly a speculator, and no doubt he exploited his business opportunities to the full.

The *Jenkins Venus* was a case in point. The original statue dating from the first or second century was missing its head and several limbs. Jenkins commissioned the leading restorer in Rome, Bartolomeo Cavaceppi, and with the aid of an assortment of spare body parts, Venus regained her beauty, to the extent that William Weddell fell in love with her and paid between one and six thousand guineas to take her back to his home at Newby Hall. Whatever the exact sum paid, it was reported that it was the highest price paid for any antiquity taken from Rome to England. Jenkins recorded that Papal permission to export the statue had been obtained only because of 'the fortunate circumstance of its being a naked female'. A rumour, allegedly originated by him, that the purchaser was the King of England, may also have helped his cause.

We know little of Jenkins' private life. He never married and had no children. The portrait opposite, painted by Angelica Kauffmann in 1790 in Rome, shows him with his niece Anna Maria in Rome. She went to live with him in 1788. According to the notes accompanying the portrait at the National Portrait Gallery:

> In 1790 she was searching for a husband and this portrait can be viewed as an advertisement of her charms. The rural setting, with distant view of the Colosseum, her white dress and the flowers she holds, all signify Anna Maria's beauty and purity. Welcoming potential suitors, her uncle takes off his hat and pats the dog - symbol of loyalty - whose collar reads 'Jenkins'. [4]

Anna Maria's surname was Martinez. In the Jenkins' family tree drawn up by Hutchinson, he indicates that William's daughter Charlotte married a Mr Martinez. Jenkins' will refers to two nieces, daughters of his brother William, Sarah and 'my dearly beloved niece, Charlotte'. Presumably Charlotte changed her name to Anna Maria at the time of her marriage.

In 1773, while still living in Rome, Jenkins began to purchase property in Devon, first Bindon, near Axmouth, and then Cotford in Sidbury. The Sidmouth Manor Estate had been in the Prideaux family since 1624: the family was deeply in debt, and the Court of Chancery ordered the sale of the Manor for the payment of creditors. It was put up for auction on 2 May, 1787 and Hutchinson records that:

> *A Mr Oliver Cromwell, a solicitor or attorney at law, who was acting for Mr Thomas Jenkins, then at Rome, bid the sum of £15,600, and the manor of Sidmouth was knocked down to him… The small sum for which it was acquired by Mr Jenkins was indeed very remarkable.*[5]

The beginning of the French Revolution in 1789 changed everything in Europe. For Thomas Jenkins it marked the end of his lucrative business in Rome, as the rich and great were no longer able to take the Grand Tour. He had to look elsewhere for business opportunities. With the trend towards the rich and famous taking seaside holidays in England, he decided on a speculative venture and commissioned the architect Michael Novosielski, whom he had met in Rome, to build a grand crescent in Sidmouth, and work began in 1790.

❧ MICHAEL NOVOSIELSKI ❧

Michael Novosielski was born into a Polish family in Rome in 1750. He moved to London as a young man to assist James Wyatt in the building of the Pantheon between 1770 and 1772. He worked as a theatrical scene painter and in 1782 he got the job of refurbishing the King's Theatre, Haymarket.

It seems that Novosielski shared Jenkins' entrepreneurial spirit. In 1785 he acquired a lease of fourteen acres of land in Kensington and the following year began construction of a terrace of forty-four houses, which he called Michael's Place in honour of himself. This was completed in 1795. He also built a mansion for himself and began work on a crescent of houses called, unsurprisingly, Novosielski Street. In the same period, following the destruction by fire of the King's Theatre in 1789, Novosielski rebuilt it as the Opera House between 1790 and 1791. It was then one of the largest theatres in Europe, second only to La Scala in Milan. He was involved with a number of other London projects including the Concert Room in Tottenham Court Road and the Earl of Barrymore's house in Picadilly. It was in the midst of all this activity that he built Fortfield Terrace in Sidmouth.

Unfortunately, Novosielski died on 8 April, 1795, and Fortfield Terrace, like many of his projects, remained uncompleted. Anna Sutton, in her book *A Story of Sidmouth,* records that 'a letter in the possession of Mrs. Crabb-Watt, dated July, 1795, from Paton to Henry Holland, a London architect, states that Jenkins Lord of the Manor of Sidmouth, was very upset because Novoselski [sic] the architect had died before the completion of his new Crescent.'[6]

All of Novosielski's creations in London were either subsequently demolished or destroyed by fire, and it may be that Fortfield Terrace alone stands as a memorial to his creative energy.

This portrait of Novosielski, painted in 1791, again by Angelica Kauffmann, shows him with his plans for the Opera House, and in the background is a terrace, which looks like a completed version of Fortfield Terrace.

MICHAEL NOVOSIELSKI *by Angelica Kauffmann*
National Gallery of Scotland

As someone who loves Italy and things Italian, I find it very pleasing to think that Fortfield Terrace may have been financed by an Italian statue of Venus, and conceived in a coffee shop in Rome.

SIDMOUTH IN 1795 *by G Rowe*   Sidmouth Museum

This is the first known engraving of Sidmouth, published by J Walker in 1796 from an original water-colour painted by G Rowe in 1795. In it, the newly built and incomplete terrace makes its first mark on the landscape of Sidmouth, a world apart from the busy cities of Rome and London.

CHAPTER TWO
HOLIDAY HOMES BY THE SEA

❧ ROYAL INFLUENCE ❧

King George III was a conscientious, if conservative, king. His reign of sixty years was the longest of any British king, and second only to Queen Victoria as British monarch. Unlike his Hanoverian predecessors, he had a genuine affection for England, and appreciated the beauty of the countryside, hence his nickname 'Farmer George'. Also, unlike his Hanoverian predecessors, he had the advantage of being a fluent English-speaker.

He was a moral and sensitive ruler, though his political methods were not always entirely constitutional. His reign was punctuated by unfortunate events over which he had little influence. There may have been some mismanagement leading to the loss of the American Colonies in 1783, but over other events he had no control, such as the French Revolution and the declaration of war by France on Britain in 1793. But his two major misfortunes were closer to home and personal.

Firstly, there was his illness, 'the Madness of King George', in 1765, 1788, 1801, 1804 and the final ten years of his life until his death in 1820. He was doubly unfortunate that his illness was treated appallingly, even by contemporary standards. Although it has been suggested that he suffered from acute intermittent porphyria, some of the features of his illness do not support this diagnosis.

Secondly, there was the behaviour of his son George, who as Prince of Wales was as extravagant and irresponsible as his father was restrained and dutiful. George Junior, of course, went on to become Regent in 1811 and King George IV in 1820. His early antics gained him the ultimate recognition alongside Beau Brummel in the series of Dandies on Players Cigarette Cards.[1]

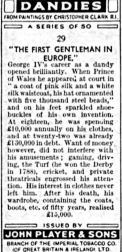

He had a long relationship with Mrs Maria Fitzherbert whom he married in 1784. Due to constitutional problems, the marriage was not recognised in law. Despite his indiscretions, George IV was also a great patron of the arts, and his regency and reign were considered to be one of the high-points of English social life.

George III and George IV influenced Sidmouth and other seaside towns in a more specific way: they popularised the English Seaside Holiday. George III's patronage of Weymouth, and George IV's of Brighton, promoted the health-giving properties of the seaside above those of the traditional spas, and encouraged the development of seaside resorts as fashionable places to stay.

> *In the 1790s the pace of development quickened, as the mild climate, scenic beauties and relatively cheap accommodation of the area became more widely known among the nobility and gentry. Sidmouth, Dawlish and Teignmouth emerged as resorts during this decade, and many of Sidmouth's visitors stayed on into the winter months. The south Devon coast was already becoming a retirement area for invalids, returned East India Company officials and half-pay officers. (Walton 1983)[2]*

Visitors started coming down from Bristol and Bath to the south Devon coast. At the first national census in 1801 the population of Sidmouth was only 1,252. However, the bandwagon was rolling, and it was in this context that the speculative development of Fortfield Terrace took place.

❧ THE FORT FIELD ❧

Prior to the building of the Terrace, the Fort Field (or Middle Field as it was then known) was farmed in narrow strips running at right angles to the sea shore, each strip identified by the name of its tenant. As late as 1795, Thomas Jenkins continued to buy land in the Fort Field: this was not Manor land, and so had to be acquired separately for his grand venture. Records at the Devon Record Office show land acquisitions from William and Elizabeth Rugg of Newton Poppleford, and from Emanuel Baruch Lousada, who lived at Peak House, then the only substantial building on the west side of Sidmouth, which also features in the 1796 etching on page 8.

The Fort Field took its name from a small fort at its southern edge. There had been a potential threat to the South Coast for centuries, both from pirates and from other nations with whom Britain happened to be at war. In 1628, with the main aggressors being the Dutch and French, the Privy Council recommended that a fort be constructed at Sidmouth and by the mid seventeenth century this had been done. In 1794 the Fort contained five pieces of ordnance, a small armoury and a flag staff. The Fort fell into disrepair after the end of the Napoleonic Wars.[3]

This watercolour of the fort was painted by Peter Orlando Hutchinson and appears in his *History of Sidmouth*. It is based on the memories of Mr Hugh Wheaton, the Sexton of Sidmouth Parish Church.

THE FORT *by Peter Orlando Hutchinson*
West Country Studies Library

✍ CONSTRUCTION OF THE TERRACE ✍

We have no historical details about the construction of the Terrace. It was built mainly of brick, rather than the more expensive stone. Foundations were shallow and there was no damp-proofing, with stone floors in the basements and wooden floors above. Internally, the houses were arranged typically for the time, with the main drawing room at first floor level, the dining room at ground floor level and the kitchen and service rooms in the basement. The servants' quarters would have been in the attic floor. Despite the conversion of most of the houses into apartments in the twentieth century, some of the original features remain, such as the ornate cornicing and hardwood staircase handrails with spiral ends.

Externally, many of the architectural features of the time are apparent, with semicircular fanlights above the front doors, sash windows of various ages, doric columns and iron railings. The first-floor balcony at No 8 has the original Georgian ironwork. From quite an early stage, the external brickwork on some of the houses was whitewashed, while others remained untreated. It was not until the 1870s that the Terrace achieved a uniform white stucco façade.

Rainwater drainage at the front still runs into the original soakaways, while at the back of the Terrace, the wells which supplied water until the 1890s were obliterated by the installation of Victorian plumbing. There is still an original ice-house at the rear of No 8.

Just as it would today, business began while the Terrace, originally known as 'the Crescent', was still being built. The original legal documents held at the Devon Record Office reveal the identity of the first lease-holders, and possibly residents, of the Crescent. It is interesting to see how some of these early names recur through the next 100 years of Sidmouth's history.

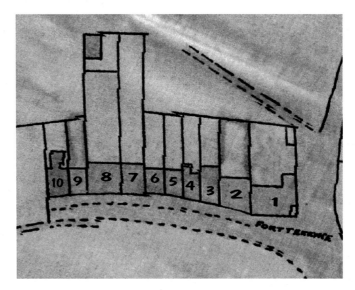

PLAN OF FORT TERRACE
adapted from early plan

The first recorded lease of the Crescent at the Devon Records Office shows that in 1795 **No 6** was leased by Thomas Jenkins of Rome to Joanna Gerrard Fulford (widow) of Devon (age approximately 39). Mrs Fulford had married into the Fulford family of Fulford Manor, Dunsford (on the road between Exeter and Moretonhampstead), in Devon. The lease was a 'Tenancy for two lives', the lease to be continued by Joanna's daughters, Elizabeth Mary (then aged 20) and Florence Ann (15). The cost was £420 with an annual rent of one shilling. The property was described as being 'to the East of the Colonnade', with a right of access through the colonnade to the rear of the property. The 'colonnade' is actually two doric columns screening the front door, so it is more correctly called a 'portico'.

Also in 1795, Jenkins leased **No 7** to Elizabeth Powys Floyd (spinster) of Sidmouth for £324 on similar terms to No 6, except that this was a tenancy for 'One life'. This property was described as 'to the West of the Colonnade', with access through.

Shropshire Archives show that on the death of Mary Floyd of St John's Hill, Shrewsbury in 1782, she left to her son Major John Floyd of Light Horse her house, with half the furniture, linen, plate and china. The other half of the house contents she left to her daughter, Elizabeth Powys Floyd. Mary stipulated that her friend Sarah Reynolds be allowed to live in the house for the remainder of her life, and that Elizabeth should also live there while she was unmarried, 'unless otherwise agreed'.

We do not know what was agreed, but we know that John went off to serve in the British Army in India, and the records show that in early 1796, Elizabeth Powys Floyd and Sarah Reynolds were both living in Sidmouth, presumably at No 7. Elizabeth later built Powys Cottage (in which she was living in the 1820s) and Witheby, both substantial houses in Sidmouth. She was not the last of her family to live in Fortfield Terrace, as we shall see later.

In February 1797 Thomas Jenkins leased **No 8** to Elizabeth Spicer (widow) of Bath. This was on a lease as a 'Tenant for absolute term' of 61 years, for £1,200 and an annual rent of four shillings and sixpence. The £1,200 was payable to the Rev William Jenkins of Sidmouth, Thomas' eldest nephew, who was the Vicar of Sidmouth. The property was described as comprising a dwelling and garden (110 feet x 40 feet) lying within 'the Crescent' and next to the property owned by 'Mrs Elizabeth Powys Floyd'. The property was not complete at that time, as Jenkins had yet to build the Colonnade to the west of No 8, so some construction must have continued after the death of the architect in 1795.

It seems likely that Elizabeth Spicer was the wife of William Spicer of Wear, who during his career was MP for Exeter and High Sheriff of Devon. Elizabeth had previously been married to Thomas Baring, and her sister Anne was married to Thomas' brother John: the Baring family owned Courtlands at Exmouth. At the Devon Records Office there is a letter written by Elizabeth Spicer to her brother-in-law John Baring from Sidmouth in 1806.

In 1797 Thomas Jenkins leased **No 2** to Stucley Lucas Esq of Barons Down in Somerset as a 'Tenant for absolute term' of 60 years. Interestingly, in the 1851 census, Stucley Lucas of Barons Down, presumably his grandson, is recorded as being a Fox Hunter by occupation: in an ironic twist, Barons Down is now the headquarters of the League Against Cruel Sports.

At around this time **No 9** was leased to F Coleman Esq as a 'Tenant for one life' with an annual rent of one shilling.

Rev William Jenkins, Thomas' nephew, was the 'Tenant at will' of **Nos 1, 3, 4, 5 and 10**. He was an interesting character in his own right. In *Trewman's Exeter Flying Post* of 14 March, 1787 it is recorded that

> Last week a Dispensation passed the Great Seal, to enable the Rev William Jenkins MA, late Fellow of Sidney College, Cambridge, and Chaplain to His Royal Highness the Duke of Cumberland, and also to the Rt Hon Lord Viscount Maynard, to hold the vicarage of Sidmouth, together with the Rectory of Northleigh, in the County of Devon, and Diocese of Exeter.[4]

Perhaps it was just coincidence that one month later, his uncle in Rome bought the Manor of Sidmouth. In 1810 Rev William Jenkins was living at Salcombe House (now the Hunter's Moon Hotel) and letting the vicarage (in Temple Street) as a lodging-house. In those days the 'Care of Souls' was obviously a profitable business.

❧ FROM JENKINS TO JENKINS ❧

The following representation of the Jenkins family tree is based on Peter Orlando Hutchinson's version in his *History of Sidmouth*[5] with some information from other sources.

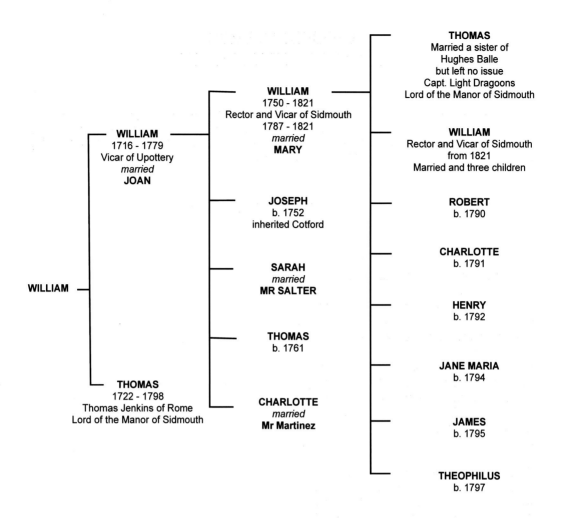

In the spring of 1798 Thomas Jenkins left Rome to return to England. It could be that at the age of 76 he felt the need to return to the land of his birth. He may have been in declining health, as he had seen it necessary to make his will the previous year. But most likely his decision would have been mainly influenced by the threat of the French army under Napoleon Bonaparte, which had invaded Northern Italy and was advancing towards Rome.

Because of this, he was forced to return by sea. He was taken ill on the voyage home, and died on 11 May after landing at Great Yarmouth. As far as we know he never saw the estate he had purchased or the terrace he had commissioned.

On the death of Thomas Jenkins, the Manor of Sidmouth, and hence the ownership of Fortfield Terrace, passed to his great nephew, also Thomas Jenkins. According to Hutchinson, the will was in Italian, poorly written, and disputed: when translated from Italian, the wording regarding the titles to property was invalid under English law.

So Fortfield Terrace was conceived and built: seaside homes for the gentry and, occasionally, the aristocracy. Over the next century this community was to change gradually, as Sidmouth itself developed, reflecting the changing face of society.

CHAPTER THREE
GEORGIAN ELEGANCE

Despite being at war with France, Britain entered the nineteenth century in a comfortable and optimistic state. In many ways its architecture symbolised its society: practical and solid, but at the same time well-proportioned and graceful, it spoke of a comforting solidity and security allied to style and elegance.

❧ JANE AUSTEN ❧

JANE AUSTEN *after Cassandra Austen*
National Portrait Gallery, London

Sidmouth was becoming a fashionable place to stay, and the first of its notable visitors of the nineteenth century was Jane Austen. It is frustrating that we know so little about this phase of her life. There are particular reasons for this. She was not famous at this stage, so any information has to be gleaned from within the family. After Jane's death, Cassandra, her elder sister to whom most of Jane's letters were written, destroyed many of them to protect her memory from prying eyes.

Tantalisingly, the only factual evidence we have is of the Austen family's intention to spend the summer in Sidmouth in 1801, shortly after they had moved to Bath. Comments made by Cassandra towards the end of her life to her nephews and nieces suggest that while in Sidmouth, Jane fell in love for the one and only time with a young gentleman who may have been a clergyman. He had to leave Sidmouth to fulfil an engagement, and it was anticipated that he would return immediately to rejoin the Austens. Sadly, shortly after this, the Austens received a letter from his brother saying that he had died suddenly.[1]

We can only speculate as to whether Jane Austen and her family stayed in Fortfield Terrace that summer. It would have been an appropriate place for members of the country gentry to make their summer home. There are a number of possible connections. It may be that Jane's father, the Rev George Austen, was acquainted with the Rev William Jenkins. Or possibly there was some connection with Elizabeth Spicer through common acquaintances in Bath. We shall probably never know, though we live in hope of finding a hidden letter, or uncovering a piece of graffiti saying 'Jane was here'.

Her unfinished novel, *Sanditon*[2], is about a small seaside town, speculative development and even a 'short row of smartlooking Houses, called the Terrace with a broad walk in front'. She writes, as the story unfolds:

> *The Terrace was the attraction to all; Every body who walked, must begin with the Terrace & there, seated on one of the two Green Benches by the Gravel walk, they found the united Denham Party.*

The large end house of the Terrace also features in the story. For those of us who would very much like Jane Austen to have stayed here, the fact that Sanditon was on the Sussex coast and had a sandy beach will not deter us. No doubt when she was staying in Sidmouth she would at least have walked along the gravelled pavement. Perhaps she sat on one of those green benches by the gravel walk talking to a young gentleman who may have been a clergyman. It would be nice to think that, as she sat down to write in her little room at Chawton towards the end of her life, she had some fond and perhaps wistful memories of her summer holiday in Sidmouth fifteen years before.

❧ A DEVELOPING WATERING-PLACE ❧

Like Sanditon, Sidmouth continued to develop as a resort. On 20 October, 1803 the Rev Edmund Butcher, subsequently resident at 9 Fortfield Terrace, wrote:

> *Since Sidmouth has been growing into fame as a watering-place, a great number of new houses have been erected. This very year has added no less than seven to the number; and still the Crescent, which is a row of houses called the Fortfield, remains unfinished. The houses on the western cliff are so much detached and elevated, that I think if a few more were added, they might assume the appellation of Clifton.*

These words were quoted in *Lethaby's Sidmouth Journal and Directory* of 1 April, 1864. As a footnote to the comment about the Crescent, the editor added:

> *And it remains unfinished to the present date, 1864, and its former name of Crescent has been altered to that of Fortfield Terrace.*[3]

The Crescent is still unfinished, and the houses on the western cliff did become Clifton.

Development was unregulated and had no overall plan, as was the case with many seaside resorts. As Walton says:

> *This manner of development produced results which satisfied the architectural and spatial requirements of most resort users, whether the prevailing idiom was the monumental terrace, the villa or the cottage ornée. There were exceptions. In 1799 G S Carey found Margate's streets narrow and filthy, remarking that its Parade had 'little to boast of in respect to elegance or even cleanliness'; and 30 years later, Blackpool too was found to be lacking in architectural dignity: 'It is a pity but [there should have] been some kind of uniformity observed, as all sea bathing places ought to have there houses built on a plan entirely unique.' These were unusual cases, and the widely prevailing taste for the picturesque and romantic ensured that the second comment expressed a far from universal perception. Sidmouth, for example, was described as 'generally neat, occasionally highly picturesque, and in some parts positively handsome', despite being 'irregularly built'.*[4]

As part of this process, in 1806 Lord Gwydir, the Deputy Lord Great Chamberlain, bought Old Hayes (now the Woodlands Hotel) and began to convert it into a cottage ornée. The Cottage Ornée style, popular between 1730 and 1820, took the traditional rustic cottage, and embellished it with ornate elements, often gothic.

A few years later, Lord and Lady Le Despenser started to build Knowle Cottage (subsequently the Knowle Hotel and now the offices of East Devon District Council). The particular significance of these events to our story is that according to Hutchinson both Lord Gwydir and Lady Le Despenser stayed at No 1 Fortfeld Terrace, the large end house of the Terrace, while works were in progress.

Also in 1806, Stucley Lucas assigned the residue of the lease of No 2 (for 'a dwellinghouse, garden, coach house, stables and premises') to Messrs William Robins, John Newberry and Samuel Pile, who in turn leased the coach house and stables to Peter, Lord Gwydir, for £21.

❧ THE FIRST ROYAL VISITOR ❧

It was the involvement of Lord Gwydir that led to the first royal visit to the Terrace. As we have seen, the Prince of Wales (to become George IV) was leading a fairly unrestrained lifestyle and he was heavily in debt. In 1795 he married his cousin, Princess Caroline of Brunswick, this time with the approval of church and state. This was entirely a marriage of expediency: George hoped that by so doing he would gain the approval of Parliament to cover his debts. By the spring of 1796 they were living separately. Princess Caroline received a great deal of public sympathy for the way in which she had been treated.

CAROLINE AMELIA ELIZABETH OF BRUNSWICK
by Sir Thomas Lawrence
National Portrait Gallery, London

Among her supporters was Lord Gwydir, and it was in the late spring of 1806 that she came and stayed with the Gwydirs at No 1 Fort Terrace. The event was documented in *Trewman's Exeter Flying Post* of 29 May, 1806.

> **Sidmouth, May 25.** *On Tuesday last her Royal Highness the Princess of Wales and suite, arrived here, on a visit to that worthy and benevolent man Lord Gwydir, and family. His Lordship, we are happy to state, is rapidly recovering from the complaint that a few months since threatened to deprive society of one of its brightest ornaments. Her Royal Highness was received with every possible mark of respect, from all descriptions of the inhabitants; the volunteer artillery fired a very correct salute of 21 guns from the fort, and at the church.*
>
> *On the following day, the Princess, attended by Lord Gwydir and his most excellent Lady Willoughby, went to view an elegant villa near the town, in the cottage style, which his Lordship is building, having determined to make this place his residence, in consequence of the benefit he has experienced from its mild and salubrious air. In the evening her Royal Highness condescended to appear at the window, and to walk along the beach parade; she expressed herself highly delighted with the romantic scenery, and the extensive sea views of this charming spot, which render it almost unequalled. Indeed from the local superiority, and the constant influx of visitors of high distinction, Sidmouth bids fair to be one of the most elegant and fashionable watering-places upon this part of the coast.*
>
> *On Thursday her Royal Highness took leave of her noble host and hostess, and of the town (highly satisfied with the flattering reception she had met with) on her way to Cussnels, the seat of G Rofe Esq. near Christchurch [Cuffnels, the seat of the Right Honourable George Rose, MP for Christchurch, near Lyndhurst]; having previously, with great politeness and consideration, declined the honour of a salute from the Fort, in consequence of the indisposition of some visitors of distinction, who are residing here for the recovery of their health.*[5]

This account not only emphasises the rapidly growing reputation of Sidmouth as a holiday resort, but also its emergence as a health resort for 'visitors of distinction', some of whom were probably staying in the Terrace.

CHAPTER FOUR
REGENCY DAYS

❧ MORE BUSINESS ❧

By 1811, when the Regency started, the population of Sidmouth had risen to 1,688. Business at the Terrace continued. In 1809 Messrs William Robins, John Newberry and Samuel Pile sold the remainder of the lease for No 2 to Edward Andrews. In 1816 the freehold of No 2 was sold by the Manor to the Rev James Hobson, along with the coach house and stables. In 1819 the lease for No 9 was assigned by Rev William Cockburn (later styled Sir William Cockbourne DD, Dean of York) to the Rev Edmund Butcher in 'a bond for quiet enjoyment of a house in the Fort Field, Sidmouth'. The same year No 9 was sold by the Manor to the Rev Edmund Butcher, who also held the lease for No 3, but lived at No 9 with his wife Elizabeth, and his son Edmund and daughter Emma. For the next half century, Nos 2 and 9 were the only parts of Fortfield Terrace not to be a part of the Manor Estate.

In 1817, No 5 Fortfield Terrace was leased by Samuel Frederick Milford (of Exeter) and Thomas Jenkins (late Captain in 11th Regiment of Light Dragoons) to George White of Sidmouth (Captain White RN) for 7 years. Hutchinson treated Thomas Jenkins (Junior), the Lord of the Manor of Sidmouth, and Captain in the 11th Regiment of Light Dragoons, with as much suspicion as he had treated his great-uncle. It seems that there were good grounds for this. Thomas was married to a sister of Edward Hughes Ball Hughes, the infamous 'Golden Ball'. This extraordinary character also features in the Dandies series of Players Cigarette Cards along with George IV and Beau Brummell, as well as playing a part in the subsequent history of Sidmouth.[1]

EDWARD HUGHES BALL HUGHES

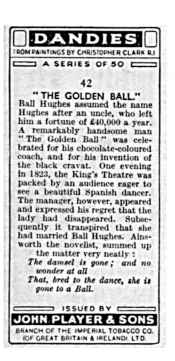

Although this relationship in itself would, in his eyes, be enough to raise Hutchinson's suspicions, the behaviour of Thomas Jenkins (Junior) towards the Manor of Sidmouth during his ownership would have confirmed them.

❧ MAKING CAPITAL ❧

From 1809 onwards, the Lord of the Manor, Thomas Jenkins (Junior), raised large sums of money by issuing leases on or selling off parts of the estate, and by taking out mortgages to raise cash. We can only assume that this was to support a life of luxury, or possibly to pay off gambling debts. At this time it appears that he was living at Sidmonton House in the County of Southampton. Apart from selling Nos 2 and 9 Fortfield Terrace, he also put up large parts of the Estate for auction on three occasions.

The first was on 8 May, 1813. The property details are all listed in a prospectus (original document at Devon Record Office), along with the names of the sitting tenants and the rents they were paying. Of particular interest to us are the listings for dwelling houses in Fort Field (the house numbers do not appear in the original document).

Tenant at Will
        Rev William Jenkins Five dwelling houses in Fortfield – [Nos 1, 3, 4, 5, 10] Present rent £360 0s 0d

Tenants for Absolute Terms
        Edward Andrews Esq, (assignee of Stucley Lucas) dwelling house in Fort Field [No 2], for 60 years from Lady Day 1798, head rent £1 3s 6d

        Rt Hon Lord Gwydir, coach house and stables (Held under the same lease with Mr Andrews, and for the same term)

        Mrs Spicer, dwelling house in Fort Field [No. 8] for 61 years from Michaelmas 1797, head rent 4s 6d.

Tenants for One Life
        F Coleman Esq, (age 73) dwelling house in Fort Field [No. 9], head rent 1s.

        Miss Floyde, (age 63) dwelling house in Fort Field [No. 7], head rent £1 1s.

        Miss Plydell, Plot of ground of several gardens and of the Fort Field, head rent £10 10s.

Tenants for Two Lives
        Mrs Fulford, (age 59) and **J A Fulford** (age 35), dwelling house in Fort Field [No. 6], head rent 1s.

There is no record of the outcome of this auction, but we can assume that the Fort Field properties were unsold, as a further sale was advertised two years later, on 10-13 November, 1815.

IMPORTANT FREEHOLD PROPERTY,
AT
Sidmouth, Devon.

Particulars and Conditions of Sale
OF
A TRULY VALUABLE & IMPORTANT
FREEHOLD ESTATE,
AND
The ROYALTY of the MANOR of SIDMOUTH,
WITH ITS
COURTS LEET AND COURTS BARON, HERIOTS, QUIT AND CHIEF RENTS;
COMMONS AND WASTE LANDS,
AND ALL ITS PRIVILEGES, IMMUNITIES, DEODANDS, &c.
MOST DELIGHTFULLY SITUATE
AT SIDMOUTH, IN THE COUNTY OF DEVON,
Long distinguished for its Salubrity of Air, and Superiority of Sea Bathing.

The Country around is rich and fertile, and boldly featured by Nature, embracing the most Picturesque Views in the County, which are pleasingly contrasted by the transient Marine Scenery constantly presenting itself in continued Variety; A Plenitude of Field Sports and Fishing may be enjoyed, and several Packs of Harriers are kept in the Vicinity.

THIS PROPERTY IS HIGHLY IMPROVABLE,
AND COMPRISES ABOUT
SIX HUNDRED ACRES
OF RICH
ARABLE, MEADOW, and PASTURE LAND, ORCHARDS and GARDENS,
And about 250 Acres of Common and Waste Lands,
TOGETHER WITH
One Hundred & Sixty
RESIDENCES, FARM-HOUSES, DWELLINGS & COTTAGES,
STABLES AND OUT-BUILDINGS;
Nursery Ground, Shambles, Tolls of Fairs and Markets:
Let to respectable Tenants, at Rents amounting annually to upwards of THREE THOUSAND POUNDS,
BUT OF THE ESTIMATED ANNUAL VALUE OF
SEVEN THOUSAND POUNDS.

This Property, from its Locality, possesses great Capability of Improvement; desirable as a Marine Retreat, and particularly eligible to any Nobleman or Gentleman desirous of vesting Money advantageously, and of Improving his Income. The Land Tax is Redeemed, and a considerable Part of the Purchase Money may remain on Mortgage.

Which will be Sold by Auction,
BY MR. H. PHILLIPS,
AT THE
YORK HOTEL, SIDMOUTH,
On FRIDAY 10th, SATURDAY 11th, and MONDAY 13th of NOVEMBER, 1815,
At Eleven o'Clock, in One Hundred and Sixty Lots,
(UNLESS AN ACCEPTABLE OFFER SHOULD BE PREVIOUSLY MADE FOR THE WHOLE ESTATE.)

May be Viewed by application to Mr. GOULD, Solicitor, Honiton, of whom printed Particulars may be had; of Mr. SURMAN; Solicitor, Golden Square; Mr. NOWELL, Essex Street, Strand; and Mr. WARREN, New Inn, London; at the Old London Inn, Exeter; King's Arms, Dorchester; Crown, Blandford; Golden Lion, Lyme; White Hart, Salisbury; Dolphin, Southampton; CRUTWELL, Printer, Bath; of the Printer of the Bristol Mercury; LANGDON and SON, Sherborne; Printer of the Cheltenham Chronicle; Fountain, Plymouth Dock; Wallis's and Marsh's Libraries, Sidmouth; at the Mart, and of Mr. PHILLIPS, No. 73, New Bond Street, London; where a Plan of the Estate may be seen.

SALE NOTICE 1815 Devon Record Office

The items of most interest to us came up on the second day of the sale, Saturday, 11 November.

Lot	House, Cottages, Lands, &c.	Present Rent		
		£	s	d
56	FORT FIELD, no rich Pasture Land, an eligible and beautiful Spot for the Erection of Marine Villas, on a rising Ground, with view of the sea	100	0	0
61	A *capacious* DWELLING HOUSE with its Domestic Offices, Cellars, &c. No. 1, Situate in FORT FIELD, with *View of the Sea.*	100	0	0
62	A Ditto and Ditto, No. 3, of lesser Dimensions	65	0	0
63	A Ditto and Ditto, No. 4	65	0	0
64	A Ditto and Ditto, No. 5	65	0	0
65	A Ditto and Ditto, No. 10	65	0	0

The land in the Fort Field was presumably that which Thomas Jenkins Senior had bought for his Crescent: there seems to be a tacit acceptance that the Crescent would never be finished. The houses in the Terrace were the properties where there were no sitting tenants, the leaseholder being William Jenkins.

Finally, a sale was held in 1819, with an advertisement similar to the previous one, documented in Hutchinson's *History of Sidmouth*:[2]

> In 1819 there was an advertisement in a newspaper concerning the Manor of Sidmouth. It reads as follows: 'Important Freehold Property, Sidmouth, Devon, by Mr. Phillips, at the York Hotel, Sidmouth on Thursday the 26th Instant and two following days at eleven and noon, in 156 lots. A truly valuable and important estate, and the Royalty of the Manor of Sidmouth, comprising about six hundred acres of arable, meadow and pasture land, orchards and gardens, and about 250 acres of common and waste lands, together with upwards of one hundred and sixty residences, farm houses, cottages, stables and extensive buildings, nursery grounds, shambles, tolls of fairs and markets, let to respectable tenants at annual rents amounting to upwards of three thousand pounds, but of the estimated value of seven thousand pounds. The Estate is capable of considerable improvement, as is desirable as an investment of money, and improvement of income. The Land Tax is redeemed.'

> [Margin note in *History of Sidmouth*] 'Since this was written, Miss Lester, who has a lease of 8 Fortfield Terrace, where she resides, has sent me the large advertisement of the proposed auction, issued by the auctioneer, and occupying twelve folio pages of printed matter. It contains a list of the tenants under the Manor; description of property, nature of property leases, and in short, all particulars for the entire dismemberment of the Manor.'

Following the end of the Napoleonic Wars, times were difficult financially: it seems unlikely that these attempted sales were very successful, and with the exception of Nos 2 and 9, Fortfield Terrace remained within the ownership of the Manor.

from **THE LONG PICTURE OF SIDMOUTH** *by Hubert Cornish 1815*   Sidmouth Museum

✄ A SALUBRIOUS SPOT ✄

War with France ended in 1815, and England was left to enjoy the Regency Period.

The picture on the previous page shows the Terrace as part of a panoramic series of three, painted by Hubert Cornish in 1815, commonly known as 'the Long Picture of Sidmouth'. It gives a romantic glimpse into a comfortable life; at least for the better off. Even the dogs seem at ease.

In his *History of Sidmouth*, Hutchinson comments on some of the inaccuracies in this series of pictures, but reminisces about the scene shown above:

> The road starting from the beach near Fort Cottage, and running away across the field to the large white house, I can well remember. This road was stopped and grassed over when the field was enclosed with iron railings: but even now, sometimes in dry summer weather, its course may be traced.[3]

There was obviously a bit of artistic licence, as Hutchinson says, including the placing of the balcony incorrectly on No 7 Fortfield Terrace instead of No 8.

In *The Beauties of Sidmouth Displayed* (1820), the Rev Edmund Butcher, a Fortfield Terrace resident, writes:

> In the flat part of the valley, west of the town, and open to the sea, a row of brick houses appear, in number eleven, which, if finished according to the plan laid down, would form a crescent with a small curve. No 4 is the residence of Misses Schimmelpenninck; No 5 Capt White RN; and No 6. Mrs Fidford. The rest are let for hire. The field they stand in is called the Fort-Field...[4]

Trewman's Exeter Flying Post of 1 January, 1818 records the death of the widow of William Spicer, MP Exeter Topsham, better known to us as Elizabeth Spicer, leaseholder of No 8 Fort Terrace.[5]

✄ A PLACE OF HEALING ✄

Cornish's picture also shows the archetypal invalid in a bath chair taking the curative sea air. The Rev Butcher comments:

> Lodgings are numerous, and may be had of almost all sizes and prices, as well as in a variety of situations. They are scattered in every part of the town and its vicinity. Those on the beach, and on the Fort-Field, possessing an unbroken view of the sea are generally the most sought after. In the town, however, as more sheltered, invalids are often ordered to reside; and one great advantage of Sidmouth is, that almost every want of this sort may be supplied. Situations open or sheltered, in the sunshine or the shade, public or private, may be obtained.

He also had firm views on the healthy way of going about sea bathing:

Those persons who are fond of swimming, or prefer bathing without the use of a machine, should be informed, that a little to the west of the beach, there is a fine sequestered bay, in which they may, in calm weather, be safely gratified. The border is a fine sand; upon which, at high water, the bather may walk for a long distance out, without being immersed higher than the breast. While it is our duty to acquaint visitors of this acquisition, it is our first wish to recommend the use of Machines; both for the benefit of the proprietors and the bather, particularly the invalid. The plunge into the element should assuredly supersede the practice of walking in by degrees. "Sea bathing," says Dr Buchan, "is good for one reason, because the sea is a cold bath. The time of bathing ought to be postponed till past noon, or at least till some hours after breakfast, when the digestion of that meal may be supposed to be terminated; and such a degree of exercise should always be taken previously to entering the water, as may be sufficient to produce a sensation of a warmth over the whole body. By no means go into the water chilly".

It was to take the healthy sea air and tepid sea water baths that the Duke and Duchess of Kent arrived on Christmas Eve 1819, with the seven month old Princess Victoria. They stayed at Woolbrook Cottage, now the Royal Glen Hotel, just across the field from Fortfield Terrace. The story relates that a small boy catapulted a stone which went through the window of the bedroom in which the baby Princess was sleeping, narrowly missing her: had it not missed, the subsequent course of British and world history could have been very different. It is likely that during their stay the royal visitors walked along the Terrace. Sadly, two weeks later, the Duke developed pneumonia, and he died at Woolbrook Cottage on 23 January, 1820. Six days later King George III died. These events heralded the end of an old era, and the promise of a new.

The full title of the Rev Edmund Butcher's guide to Sidmouth, written that year is:

THE BEAUTIES OF SIDMOUTH DISPLAYED being A Descriptive Sketch of its Situation, Salubrity, and Picturesque Scenery. Also an Account of the Environs within fifteen miles round, interspersed with authentic anecdotes.

Any book with such an idiosyncratic title deserves to be widely read. It closes with following advertisements:

SEDAN AND BATH CHAIRS
Are kept by Wm. Rugg, and R. Puddicombe, J and R
Bartlet,
W. Radford and T. Silley, &c.

BATHING MACHINES
Kept by Marmaduke Taylor and Thomas Heffer, for
gentlemen.
Terms of bathing, One Shilling first time and
Sixpence each time after.
By Mrs Barrett and Co for ladies.
One Shilling and Sixpence first time and 1s. each
time after.

HORSES may be hired of B. Butler, Painter; Wm. Gove, Grocer &c.; Wm. Gale, Linen Draper; Dunsford and Hill, Saddlers; H. Smith, who have quiet and manageable Donkies, with proper saddles for invalids; both the latter supply Asses' milk.

A VIOLIN, &c.

Parties desirous of making a dance at short notice, will be waited upon by James Barnard, near the Post Office.

THE END

From time to time on Saturday mornings the sound of a violin may still be heard in the Market Place, near the old Post Office.

CHAPTER FIVE
THE GEORGIAN FINALE

➷ KING GEORGE IV ↶

King George IV was proclaimed ruler in his own right on 31 January, 1820. His reign began inauspiciously with a severe attack of pleurisy followed by the return of his wife, Princess Caroline, from another life in Italy and Germany. This happened in the midst of demonstrations, at times violently repressed, for reform of the voting system and universal suffrage. Against this background, Caroline received a good deal of public support, mainly because of the unpopularity of George. There was considerable heated debate in parliament as to what Caroline's title should be when George became king (some things don't seem to change much from one century to the next). The arguments, however, proved largely academic. George's coronation was a lavish affair: it took place in July, 1820, and three weeks later, Caroline, Queen-Consort, Fortfield Terrace's first official Royal Visitor, died after a short illness.

➷ MEANWHILE, BACK IN SIDMOUTH ↶

The 1821 census record shows that the population of Sidmouth had risen to 2,747. Over the next decade there was an influx of wealthy residents to south coast resorts: construction was continuing on a large scale in towns such as Brighton, where imposing terraces of that time dominate much of the sea front today. Development also included smaller and less accessible towns such as Lyme Regis and Sidmouth. By 1831 elite groupings (capitalists, bankers, professionals and other educated men) made up 6.25 percent of the male population of Sidmouth:[1] by then the total population of Sidmouth had risen to 3,126. During the 1820s large houses such as Sidmount were built, as were clusters of luxury villas such as those in Elysian Fields.

In the great storm of 1824, Chit Rock, the rocky outcrop by the rock pools which for centuries had been one of Sidmouth's landmarks, and which appears in the Sidmouth engraving of 1796, disappeared overnight. Even things which seem so permanent cannot withstand the force of time and change. The fact that over the years it had been used as target practice for the cannons located at the fort probably did not help.

This decade of the Terrace's history is not particularly well documented. We know that in 1821, William Jenkins, Vicar of Sidmouth and leaseholder of a large part of Fort Terrace (as the Terrace was then known), died. He was succeeded as Vicar of Sidmouth by his son, also William.

Peter Orlando Hutchinson gives us a couple of insights into Terrace life at the time.[2] As we saw in the last chapter, he recalls that in 1827 the Fort Field was enclosed with iron railings, although the Cricket Club itself was founded in 1823.

Before this time it was an open space or play ground, where sheep occasionally fed, and where children played ball, and children of a larger growth play cricket or football. From the large house of Fort Field Terrace (being Nos. 7 and 8) and intended originally to have been the grand central feature of a crescent, there took a road (made I believe when the houses were built) across the field down to the beach… [This observation is confirmed in the 1815 painting by Cornish].

Indeed, in 1827, following due legal process, the road was moved, as shown on this map.

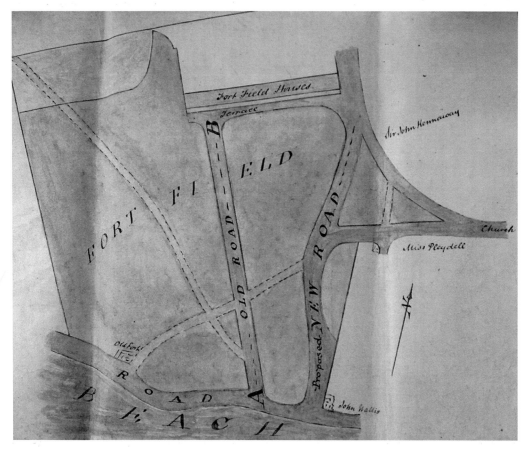

MAP OF THE FORT FIELD 1827   Devon Record Office

On the subject of cricket and Terrace life in general Hutchinson recalls:

I remember being in the Fort Field one day, when there were a number of people there witnessing the progress of a game of cricket. It may have been a little before or a little after it had been enclosed. The late Mr Spicer, then of Courtlands on the banks of the River Exe, was residing temporarily at No 8 Fortfield Terrace, and he came cantering into the field on horseback. He said in my hearing that he would not go upon the part reserved for cricket, but as tenant of that house he had a right which he wished to maintain.

This would most likely be William Frederick Spicer of Courtlands, Withycombe Rawleigh (Exmouth). He was the son of Elizabeth Spicer, who held the first lease at No 8. As far as I know no recent Terrace residents have asserted their right to ride horses on the Fort Field.

ASSORTED TERRACE RESIDENTS

As we saw in the previous chapter, the Rev Edmund Butcher names some of the long-term residents of the Terrace in 1820.

No. 4 Fort Terrace was occupied by the Misses Schimmelpenninck. This is a Dutch family name. Notable Schimmelpennincks of the time included Rutger Jan Schimmelpenninck who was the Batavian (Dutch) ambassador to Britain in 1802 and 1803 and Grand Pensionary (Governor) of the Batavian Republic in 1805. He was also a member of the senate of the Kingdom of the United Netherlands between 1815 and 1820 and had a cigar named after him in 1995. Then there was Mary Anne Schimmelpenninck (née Galton) who married a Dutch trader, Lambert Schimmelpenninck in 1806. He had commercial links with the West Indies and was a partner in a firm which invested in African slavers from Bristol. Interestingly, as well as being a literary theorist, theologian and biographer of Erasmus Darwin, Mary was an ardent campaigner against slavery. We do not know if our ladies were related to either of these. We do however know that in 1841 Anna Schimmelpenninck, age 60, was living at No 3 with her two servants. It seems that residents quite often moved from one house to another within the Terrace, particularly between properties belonging to the same landlord.

The Rev Butcher's 'Mrs Fidford' at No 6 is presumably Mrs Joanna Fulford, the original leaseholder, now 64 years old. We shall come across the Rev Butcher and Mrs Fulford later in this book.

One family of Terrace residents had a particularly good local pedigree: the Coplestons of Offwell. They had a presence in the Terrace for most of the nineteenth century.

THE COPLESTONS

John Bradford Copleston (born 1749) became Rector of Offwell, near Honiton, in 1774. He was married to Margaret Gay, and they had six children, all born at Offwell: Edward (born 1776), John Gaius (born 1778) both of whom succeeded their father as Rector of Offwell, Frances (born 1781), Ann (born 1782), James (born 1787) and Caroline (born 1789). It is most likely that the Rev J Copleston known to be living at Old Hayes (now the Woodlands Hotel) in Sidmouth around 1800 was the Rev J B. Following this, he and his wife went to live in Exeter.[3]

Ann died in 1804 at the age of 22. James, a lieutenant in the Royal Artillery was lost at sea on route to Gibraltar in 1812. We do not know when Frances and Caroline moved to Sidmouth. We do know that they lived in 1, 1½ and 3 Fortfield Terrace for much of their adult lives. They were both unmarried, and appear in the town residents' lists of the 1840s as 'the Misses Copleston'.

Edward was the famous member of the family. He studied at Corpus Christi College, Oxford, and went on to become Professor of Poetry at Oxford University. In 1811 he was instrumental in the expulsion of the poet Shelley from Oxford University, for the writing of a pamphlet entitled *The Necessity of Atheism*. In 1814 he became Provost of Oriel College, at which time he became a Doctor of Divinity. He was well known for his writings in defence of Oxford scholarship.

His career in the church was equally impressive. Rector of Offwell from 1800 to 1804 and then Vicar of St Mary's, Oxford, in 1812 he became prebendary of Huxton in St Paul's Cathedral, and in 1826 Dean of Chester. In 1827 he was made Bishop of Llandaff and Dean of St Paul's. The diocese of Llandaff at that time consisted of Monmouthshire and most of Glamorgan. As Bishop of Llandaff he was instrumental in promoting the restoration of the Church in Wales, making sure that the clergy he appointed were able to speak Welsh. During his time as Bishop, twenty new churches were built in the diocese.

EDWARD COPLESTON DD
Llandaff Cathedral

But he is particularly interesting to us as a family man, with a deep respect for his parents and devotion to his brother and sisters.

> *By nature as well as name, too, as Dr Copleston often pleasantly tells us, his mother was Gay and cheerful. She lived till she was 92, and retained to the last her constitutional cheerfulness and good humour. His father had died seven years before.*[4]

His appreciation of 'family' comes across in a letter he wrote about a Sunday at Offwell:

> 9 Nov, 1828 *My father and his grandson John served the Church in the morning. My brother read prayers and I preached in the afternoon. The remarkable union of three generations in my native place made a strong impression on us all and upon the whole parish. Only two individuals of the congregation were there whom my father found at his first coming to Offwell in 1774.*[5]

It is in his letters to his two sisters at Fortfield Terrace,[6] of which we have four, that we find him at his most honest, witty and warm. In the first, written from Oriel College, Oxford, on 12 July, 1818, he talks amusingly about his introduction to a Dr Cleve, who intended to start teaching in Exeter:

> *He appears to be a modest, warmhearted, conscientious man – but his dialect is one of the worst specimens that could be heard even within his own college, which he calls Beliol. It partakes of the peculiarities of the*

more cultivated classes about Ottery and Honiton – not a single vowel being pronounced as Englishmen in general speak – altho' in the course of a few minutes conversation you hear all the vowel sounds of our language, only transferred to syllables where you don't expect them. Without any affectation I must say that it often required time and reflection to ascertain the meaning, and I was heartily glad that no one was present whose risibility might have provoked my own.

He also talks about meeting Mrs Sarah Siddons on two or three occasions. She was one of the great tragic actresses of the time, and he commented that she:

... is a very respectable good sort of woman – and though she cannot altogether throw off the tragedy queen, seems to have no affectation of mind and is a conversible domestic personage. Her daughter who is a fine young woman and very well educated has nothing theatrical about her.

Elsewhere in the letter he asks Frances to 'thank my father for having kindly devoted so much time to penmanship to me... knowing how disagreeable an office writing is to him.'

The second letter, written from London on 3 December, 1823 was addressed to Caroline at '3 Fortfield, Sidmouth'.

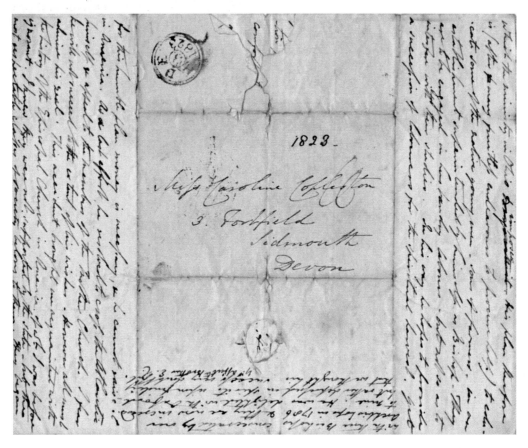

LETTER FROM EDWARD COPLESTON TO CAROLINE COPLESTON 1823
The Beinecke Rare Book and Manuscript Library
Yale University

In this letter he talks about his meeting with Mr Schlegel (August Wilhelm von Schlegel), the celebrated German author who translated Shakespeare into German, Captain Franklin, the 'distinguished adventurer' (explorer of northern Canada, later to be Sir John Franklin) and the Bishop of Ohio, whom he describes as 'a truly primitive and even Apostolic figure'. He signs the letter 'Your affectionate brother, E.C.'

Edward obviously appreciated his visits to Devon. On 5 August, 1830, now Bishop of Llandaff, he wrote to his diocesan Vicar General, Bruce Knight:

> I have spent nearly four weeks most delightfully in Devonshire, where I have three stations, Offwell, Sidmouth and Exeter.[7]

The third personal letter addressed to 'My dear sisters' was written from the Deanery, St Paul's on 25 June, 1832, the year after the death of their father. He writes that he hopes to visit Offwell the following month and 'after being there a few days shall doubtless have the pleasure of paying you and my mother a visit at Sidmouth'. He talks about having dined with the Duke of Wellington the previous Saturday. This letter is signed, 'Ever yours affectionately, E. Llandaff'. One assumes that his mother was then living with Frances and Caroline.

His health was not good and, like many before and since, he enjoyed the health-giving properties of the East Devon air, and the sanctuary of his family:

> I had a severe attack in April, & finding myself getting worse & worse, I left town for Devonshire early in May, whence after a month's residence at Offwell & Sidmouth, I returned almost well.
> letter to J M Treharne, Deanery, St Paul's, 22 June, 1835[8]

> If I do not get better I must flee for some alleviation to the society of relations – last year I recovered gradually at Sidmouth in this way – taking horse exercise in the open ground upon the hills...
> letter to Bruce Knight, 25 June, 1836[9]

The last of the four personal letters to his sisters was written from Chepstow on 1 November, 1837.[10] In this letter, addressed to Frances, he is very reflective and a little sad. He is obviously feeling the strain of work and ill health. On a practical note he says:

> Pray let me know what sums Caroline has had for the housekeeping account, since July 25, when I think she drew for £30 on Sander's Bank. Since that, I think John has sent £30 twice. I now have a sufficiency at the Exeter Bank to answer any demand she may wish to make – but probably, if I am right about John's remittance, more will not soon be wanted.

The letter closes on a wistful note:

> I can picture you and Caroline enjoying your warm house and cheerful open scene from the windows – under this stormy sky. The sense of shelter is one of our pleasures. In summer we seldom feel it. But it enters largely into the sum of human enjoyment. It is almost the only one I now enjoy...

He signs the letter 'yours affectionately, E. Llandaff', but cannot resist, as a postscript, correcting his sister: 'Remember it is Mrs Ryder - not Rhyder. Lord Bolingbroke, not Bollingbroke'.

Their mother, Margaret Gay Copleston died in 1839, and their brother John in 1841. John, as the only married member of his siblings, had more than made up for their lack of offspring by having ten of his own, leading Edward to write on 13 April, 1846:

> *I find indeed the tribe of my brother's descendants, thus nearly connected with me, becoming very numerous & possessing more claims on my aid than I had ever expected.*[11]

The death of Edward in 1849 left the Misses Copleston as the only family survivors of their generation.

You may wonder how relevant all of this is to the history of Fortfield Terrace. I think that these sorts of strange connections are what help to make the Terrace the special place that it is. We can imagine the two unmarried sisters, lives spent in East Devon, now living in Fort Terrace, Sidmouth. Imagine their pride in the eldest brother who achieved so much and who was a connection with a different world, a world of noblemen, great actresses, daring explorers, learned scholars and strange clergymen from overseas. Imagine the delight as the letters we have seen were hand-delivered to the Terrace, and no doubt read and re-read. And imagine the Bishop staying with his sisters in the Terrace from time to time, looking out of the windows at the stormy sky over the sea, and enjoying 'the sense of shelter' that he valued so much.

The census of 1841 finds Frances and Caroline, now 60 and 52, living at No 1 Fort Terrace. By 1851, the house has been divided into two, and the sisters are living at No 1½ with their three servants, Mary Anne Hutchings (house maid, 26, from Northleigh), Susan Greenslade (cook, 25, from Offwell) and Mary Anne Palmer (lady's maid, 22, from Taunton). In 1861 Frances died, and Caroline was the last surviving family member of her generation, living with a companion, Catherine Blake age 38, from Galway in Ireland, who stayed with Caroline until her death at the age of 91. *Lethaby's Sidmouth Journal and Directory* of 1 October, 1880 simply states:

> *Died Sept 8 at 1½ Fortfield Terrace, Miss Caroline Copleston, youngest sister of the late Bishop of Llandaff, in her 92nd year.*[12]

In Sidmouth Parish Church there is a memorial to Caroline, and in St Mary's Church, Offwell, a memorial to both sisters.

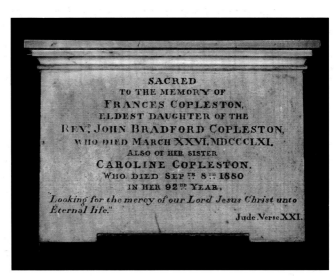

MEMORIAL TO FRANCES AND CAROLINE COPLESTON
St Mary's Church Offwell

Finally, to complete this part of the story, and to span a whole century, we read in John Tindall's *Sidmouth Chronicles* of 14 August, 1914:

> *Death of Miss (Catherine) Blake – 1½ Fortfield Terrace- aged 95 years.*
> *By her death we lose another very old and much respected inhabitant.*[13]

❧ THE END OF AN ERA ❧

In 1827, George IV left his Royal Pavilion at Brighton for the last time, and withdrew to London. He commissioned John Nash to convert Buckingham House into a palace. During this time he enjoyed the company of a number of friends, including the Duke of Wellington and the Russian Ambassador and his wife, Count and Countess Lieven. His health gradually declined and he died on 26 June, 1830.

Although his relationship with Mrs Fitzherbert had ended twenty-four years previously, she evidently remained the one real love of his life:

> *In death he remained an enigma even to those who had known him closely. Wellington told Minnie Seymour, with evident surprise, how he had noticed a miniature glittering on his sovereign's breast and found it to be a likeness of Maria Fitzherbert. It was buried with him in the vault at Windsor; and, in her house in Brighton, a grey-haired widow wept bitterly when she heard Wellington's story.*[14]

❧ KING WILLIAM IV ❧

The short reign of William IV was rather unfortunately sandwiched between the cultural glories of the Georgian era and the imperial splendour of the Victorian. He followed in the footsteps of his elder brother, George IV, by having a long affair with an Irish actress, Dorothea Bland, better known by her stage name of Mrs Jordan, by whom he had ten children. He then married Princess Adelaide of Saxe-Meiningen and had another two children, both of whom sadly died in infancy. When he was crowned in 1830 aged 64, he became the oldest ascendant to the British throne.

Having served in the Navy, he became known as the 'Sailor King'. Unlike his elder brother, William was unassuming, avoiding pomp and ceremony. During his reign the power of the monarchy was diminished, mainly due to the Parliamentary Reform Act of 1832, but other notable reforms during his reign included the reform of the Poor Law and the abolition of slavery throughout the British Empire.

In fact, quite a lot happened between 1830 and 1837, and it is unfortunate that words like 'unremarkable' and 'unimpressive' should be so often used to describe his reign. Remarkably he achieved notoriety for his habit of spitting in public, and impressively, through his liaison with Mrs Jordan, he was the ancestor of both Oliver Reed, the actor, and David Cameron, the current leader of the Conservative Party and Prime Minister.

In 1831, the year after the death of George IV, an event took place in Sidmouth which was both remarkable and impressive.

CHAPTER SIX
A ROYAL RUSSIAN VISIT

For two months in the summer of 1831, No 8 Fort Terrace achieved fame as the Imperial Residence of Grand Duchess Helena of Russia. Such a momentous event deserves a detailed account.

∂ A GRAND LADY ∽

The Grand Duchess Helena Pavlovna was the sister-in-law of the Tsars Alexander I and Nicholas I of Russia, having married their youngest brother, Michael. Interestingly, by virtue of the habitual intermarriage of the royal families of Europe, she was also the great-niece of Princess Caroline of Brunswick, whom we have already met.

Helena Pavlovna was not Russian: she was German, born Princess Charlotte Marie of Württemburg in 1807. Her early childhood was spent in Paris, where she developed a love of music, the arts and learning. She returned to Stuttgart at the age of twelve. When she was fifteen, she was selected by the Empress of Russia to be the wife of her youngest son, Michael Pavlovitch. The young girl prepared herself wholeheartedly for her new and daunting life, learning to speak and read Russian. She arrived in Russia in September 1823 and immediately won hearts.

As Catherine Drinker Bowen writes, she was 'a pretty girl of sixteen with a little round fresh face and movements so quick the Russians smiled when they saw her and asked if at home also the little Princess ran so to greet her friends'. She amazed everyone in the Russian Court by her knowledge of the country. 'When she told Karamazin, the historian, that she had read his work in the original Russian, she did not know that most Imperial ladies twice her age could digest nothing heavier than a French novel.'[1]

When she married in 1824, she became a member of the Orthodox Church and took the name of Helena (Elena) Pavlovna. Married life was not easy for Helena. The young Grand Duchess, full of the love of life and the desire to learn, was not well suited to the rigid, rather superficial, and at times sombre, atmosphere of the Russian Court. Her husband Michael was himself a frustrated man who had been sidelined into the army by his brother Nicholas.

Helena Pavlovna was a dutiful and loving wife to her husband, until his death in 1849. Her home in St Petersburg, the Michailovsky Palace, became a meeting place for artists and musicians, such as Franz Liszt and Anton Rubinstein.

> 'She was wonderful, that woman!' Rubinstein wrote. 'She looked every inch a Grand Duchess, dignified and gracious, yet she could enter completely into the mind and heart of all who approached her; an extraordinary sympathy enabled her to put herself into the most humble person's place. Scholar, statesman, artist, military man, writer, poet - upon each she made the most agreeable impression.'[2]

Apart from being a patron of the arts and founding the Russian Musical Society, Helena Pavlovna campaigned for the abolition of serfdom in Russia and was the patron of the Holy Cross Community, precursor to the Red Cross. During the Crimean War she nursed soldiers at the front, drawing comparisons with Florence Nightingale, though of course she was on 'the other side'. She died in 1873 in St Petersburg.

**GRAND DUCHESS ELENA PAVLOVNA WITH HER DAUGHTER
GRAND DUCHESS MARIA MIKHAILOVNA, 1830**
by Karl Brullov
The State Russian Museum, St Petersburg

Throughout her life she engendered affection and admiration from those she met, attracting descriptions such as 'our august and amicable Grand Duchess Helen' and leaving people 'quite charmed by her wonderful brain and wide education, her tact and friendliness'. She seems to have been a remarkable woman.

❧ WHY DID SHE COME TO BRITAIN? ☙

The size and nature of her entourage may be a clue to the significance of the visit. Apart from the Grand Duchess and her daughters, the party included Countess Nesselrode, wife of the Russian Foreign Minister, Prince Gagarin (probably Sergey Sergeevich, the Russian State Councillor), and Count Tolstoi (probably Peter Alexandrovich Tolstoi, former ambassador to Paris and then Governor of St Petersburg). If not exactly a state visit, this sounds at least like a high-powered delegation.

1831 was the year after the death of George IV, and it is likely that the political purpose of this visit was to attend the coronation of King William, due to take place in September. At this time, the Russian Royal Family was in desperate need of friends. Heavy-handed reaction to internal rebellions, and the brutal suppression of the Polish Revolt against Russian rule in 1830, had engendered a lot of ill-feeling at home and abroad. The Russian establishment was acutely aware of their unpopularity. Countess Nesselrode wrote to her husband from Sidmouth on 10 July, 1831:

> One must be living abroad to have any idea of how we are hated and harried now.[3]

In times of flagging support, a 'charm offensive' by a beautiful princess has been known to restore the popularity of more than one royal family.

❧ WHY DID SHE COME TO SIDMOUTH?

Apart from the political situation, the Grand Duchess had other reasons to be away from home and in Sidmouth in particular: she came to Sidmouth on Doctors' Orders.

One of the doctors in question was Sir Alexander Crichton FRS, who from 1804 to 1819 was the Imperial Russian Physician. He continued to have close connections with the Russian Royal Family and with the Russian Ambassador to Britain, Prince Christopher Lieven, and his wife, the Countess Dorothea, whom as we have seen were in George IV's close circle of friends. He was also involved in the medical care of Queen Caroline, George IV's wife, during her final illness.

His dealings with Grand Duchess Helena during this time are particularly well documented in a paper by John Appleby for the Royal Society.[4] There was concern at the time regarding the health of the Grand Duchess. She had had three children in quick succession: Maria (1825), Elizabeth (1826), Catherine (1827) and then another, Alexandra, born on 28 January,1831. The pregnancies and deliveries had been complicated, and Crichton was convinced that they had taken their toll on her health: so much so that he feared another pregnancy might be fatal. It was decided that she needed a rest and to take curative sea air and salt baths during her stay in Britain.

Dr Crichton dismissed Brighton ('for reasons of state'), Hastings ('too hot, and confined'), Worthing and Ramsgate ('too boring'), and so the plan to come to Sidmouth was formulated in St Petersburg by royal advisors and her personal physician, Dr Harden, and was approved by the Tsar himself.

Perhaps we should not think it strange that Sidmouth was chosen. As we have seen, for at least thirty years it had been assuming a growing reputation as a health resort for the gentry and aristocracy. It was also a very socially acceptable place to be, with London newspapers reporting its high society balls and other events.

ॐ PREPARATIONS ॐ

The first hint we have that Sidmouth and Fort Terrace were on the St Petersburg map is in a letter from Edmund Butcher Jr to his mother, owner of No 9 Fort Terrace and resident at Helens, Cotmaton Road. In the letter, dated 16 May, 1830, Edmund writes:

> If you recollect Capt Krusenstern particularly recommended the Grand Duke Michael to visit Sidmouth. I wish he had liked Helens – however if he takes No 9 even tho' the terms are low it will be better than being empty.[5]

Capt Adam Johann von Krusenstern had led the first Russian circumnavigation of the world between 1803 and 1806. At the time of this letter he was an Admiral and the Director of the Russian Naval School in St Petersburg. Whether or not Grand Duke Michael did ever visit Sidmouth, the Russian Royal Family at St Petersburg was aware of its special qualities.

On the other side of the coin, certainly at least the higher strata of British society were aware of the Grand Duchess Helena, with her marriage being reported in British newspapers, and the birth of her daughter Elizabeth in 1826 meriting an entry in *The York Herald*:

> **ST PETERSBURG, MAY 31**   *Last night an express arrived here with the news of the delivery of her Imperial Highness the Grand Duchess Helena of a daughter. This joyful event was announced to the inhabitants of the capital by a salute from the citadel, and the whole city was illuminated.*[6]

Royal visits take a lot of advanced planning, so no doubt the death of George IV in June 1830 triggered the initial plans for the visit a year later. The people of Sidmouth had plenty of warning and were eagerly anticipating the event.

> **SIDMOUTH, MAY 19**   *The houses which the Russian Consul-General (Chevalier BENKHAUSEN) has engaged for the residences of the illustrious personages on their voyage from that Court are Nos. 7, 8, 9 and 10, Fort Terrace, situated due South, according to the Consul's express instructions: No. 8 was formerly in the occupation of the late Earl of ERROL. They command a universally admired sea and land prospect, embracing the cricket-ground and new promenade, the eastern and western hills, with everything of interest passing on the water. From the accommodations afforded by them for a family of distinction, and the*

*improvements and decorations which the principal houses are undergo-
ing to render them adequate for the reception of anticipated visitors, no
doubt is entertained of this retreat being the resort of a rich galaxy of rank
and fashion, throughout the ensuing season. The Archduke Michael is
not expected as was stated in our last account, but his consort the
Archduchess Helene, so universally celebrated during her recent tour
through Italy, for her beauty and accomplishments, with the Princess
Gazarin, the Countess Nesselrode, and upwards of 49 attendants. It is
reported that a military band will be in attendance, during the sojourn of
the illustrious foreigners. Viscount Weymouth has engaged Richmond
House, in the Elysian Fields, for another year, and several villas have
been inspected for persons of distinction.*

26 May, 1831   London Morning Post [7]

Warnings were issued regarding appropriate deference, and anticipation of the visit was
heightened:

SIDMOUTH   *The Officers of His Majesty's Customs at this port have
received orders from Government to see that every mark of attention and
respect should be paid to the Grand Duchess Helen, consort of the Grand
Duke Michael, and the numerous train of Russian Nobility, who are about
to take up their residence in this delightful place for the benefits of the sea
bathing. She is conveyed by a Russian man-of-war and frigate. Her mother
is the widow of the Emperor Paul. Princess Helen is about six and twenty
years old, highly accomplished, and very beautiful.*

2 June, 1831   London Morning Post [8]

For an entertaining and first-hand account of events, we have Peter Orlando Hutchinson's
reminiscences in his *History of Sidmouth*.[9] He recalls final preparations:

*On the 13th June two carriages full of servants arrived, who proceeded to
make preparations for other parties who were to follow. On the 15th five
carriages more containing servants and attendants entered the town: and
their Russian cast of physiognomy, with sallow or swarthy skins, small
grey eyes, and high cheek bones formed a striking contrast to the ruddy
and chubby Devonshire folks who congregated to stare at them. They
were distributed in lodgings in various parts of the town.*

❧ THE VISIT ❧

The arrival of the Grand Duchess herself is recorded in *Trewman's Exeter Flying Post* of
30 June, 1831.[10]

*This illustrious personage, her three daughters, and suite, amongst whom
are the Countess Nesselrode, Madame de Tolstory, Prince Pagarin, Dr
Hurder, and Monsieur de Lobstor, first secretary, arrived at Plymouth on
Monday night…*

Despite the somewhat eccentric rendition of their names, the report tells us that they arrived
in Plymouth after a twenty-three day voyage from the Baltic port of Kronstadt, the main
port of St Petersburg, in two ships of the Russian Imperial Navy, Kyalm (a ship of the line)

and Lionelle (a frigate), on the Monday night. Red tape demanded that the ships were quarantined until clearance arrived from London on the Thursday evening. At this point:

> ...Thomas Wright, Esq. and other officers of his Majesty's Customs, accompanied by J. Hawker, Esq. the Russian Consul at this port, W. H. Tonkin, Esq., Consul for the port of Exeter, and Mr. Bellamy, surgeon, immediately repaired on board, and were received by her Royal Highness in the most affable manner...

On the Friday, 24 June, the red carpet was laid out, presentations of local dignitaries were made, and the royal party boarded carriages and departed for Sidmouth via Exeter, where they stopped only to change horses on the Sidmouth Road in the evening.

The arrival of the Grand Duchess had a major impact on Sidmouth and its residents. Hutchinson goes on to recall:

> Altogether, there were nearly, if not quite, a hundred Russians located in Sidmouth at this period. The inhabitants had done much to enliven and decorate the place. A royal salute was fired at the Preventive Station, a band of music played in the Fort Field, a large arch of laurel spanned the road opposite No 1 at the entry to the Terrace, and numerous Russian flags floated everywhere. Heraldically speaking, the flags bore – Argent, a saltier azure.

LAUREL ARCH AT FORTFIELD TERRACE 1831 Sidmouth Museum

The event achieved national coverage.

> **SIDMOUTH**   For some time past great preparations had been making at this place in consequence of the engagement of a residence for the Grand Duchess Helene of Russia, and the anticipation of numerous distinguished personages, whose arrival the presence of her Imperial Highness will doubtless command. The principal lodging houses have undergone improvement. The places of public amusement and resort

have been much decorated, and the inhabitants have united in the support of a brass band of twelve performers, who will play three evenings a week from the present time to the close of October. The illustrious lady is of the most affable and engaging manner, quite easy of access, and is daily riding in her carriage, or on donkeys with the young princesses, in the town and suburbs, and may frequently be seen walking on the esplanade as early as nine or 10 o'clock in the morning. She is delighted with the situation, and expresses her high gratification at the attentions which have been shown her; several of the nobility and gentry have called on her, to whom she has expressed a wish and intention of visiting them also. Prince Lieven is daily expected, and the ensuing month will doubtless be unusually gay, but the tradesmen generally have entered into a resolution not to enhance prices of commodities; and accommodations, suitable for all ranks, may be engaged on the usual terms.

2 July, 1831   London Morning Post [11]

The text associated with the blue plaque at No 8 Fortfield Terrace commemorating the event reflects the general excitement in Sidmouth:

…Her Russian House Band, resplendent in the uniforms of her house-hold – long tunics tied with sashes and pantaloons tucked into high boots – when not required by their employer played below the balcony of No 8 Fortfield Terrace to an audience promenading on the Fortfield, or seated on benches…[12]

as is shown in this contemporaneous sketch.

THE RUSSIAN HOUSE BAND *by Walter Rees*   Julia Creeke Collection

The Grand Duchess created an immediately favourable impression, as Hutchinson relates:

> During her residence here, and after the first curiosity had passed off, the Grand Duchess, in a plain bonnet and shawl, attended by one lady, would walk about unsuspected, and visit the cottages in the neighbourhood. One day when I was out taking a stroll, I observed her issue from a cottage with her attendant, and walk on. When I arrived at the spot, the woman living in the cottage had come to the door and was looking out. Another living near, had found out who the strangers were, and informed the first who her visitor had been… "Well, to be sure!" I heard her exclaim, "Who would have thought it had been such a grand lady."

Hutchinson's father was not quite able to match her sensitivity:

> On Tuesday the 28th my late father MD, MRCP, FRS was presented to her by the Prince Gargarine, apparently her Master of Ceremonies. This Prince Gargarine was a very gentlemanly man, both in appearance and manner: and having a fresher colour complexion than most of his countrymen, was not unlike an Englishman in style. After several weeks had elapsed, and the formality had been laid aside, my father, one day in conversation about races, nations and nationality with the Prince, playfully told him he was not unlike an Englishman in appearance. But I heard my father say afterwards, when he detailed the anecdote to my mother at home, that he did not appear to relish the compliment, judging by a slight shade that momentarily passed over his countenance.

Medical attention from Dr Crichton meant that Helena's holiday by the seaside was rather restricted, as this letter dated 29 July from Crichton to Prince Lieven suggests:

> I make her Breakfast and dine alone, on a little soup, and one chop of meat, no jellies, creams nor ices nor any desert.

Even pony-riding was not entirely successful, as 'the Grand Duchess is too nervous to be able to guide it, if powny [sic] chooses to eat, drink or have any will of its own'. The rest of her entourage, however, seemed to be having a good time, as 'the nerves of the rest of the Suite do not appear to trouble them much'![13]

Indeed, a good time was had by all.

> **SIDMOUTH**   The Ball at Hetherington's London Hotel on Wednesday last was most fashionably attended; upwards of 140 distinguished individuals honoured it with their presence, among whom were Prince Gagarine and several of the Russian Nobleman and Gentlemen in the suite of the Grand Duchess. The room was beautifully and tastefully chalked with the English and Russian Arms, and superbly decorated with a magnificent profusion of luxuriant flowers, and the Ball went off with so much éclat that it is proposed that another shall take place at the above Hotel in the course of ten days, when the Grand Duchess and her Ladies of Honour will attend. On Wednesday evening his Royal Highness Prince Paul, the Duchess's illustrious father, and brother to the king of Wirtemberg, arrived at Stone's Hotel.
>
> **11 July, 1831   London Morning Post** [14]

As the days went by, the Doctor was not entirely happy with Sidmouth, on account of its 'too relaxing atmosphere', and suggested that she should 'withdraw from sea air altogether' until her liver recovered, proposing Cheltenham as an alternative.

Even if medical treatment was not progressing as had been hoped, there was no let-up in diplomatic effort. Hutchinson recalls a grand reception: this is his account of it.

> On Monday the 11th of July, The Grand Duchess held a reception or levée which was attended by most of the residents then in Sidmouth. My father took me, though I ought to have been at school. Nevertheless this, his indiscretion, enables me to describe what I saw.

I presume that this event took place at 8 Fort Terrace. As Hutchinson was twenty-one years old at the time, one wonders if his memories of himself on this occasion were entirely accurate.

> We went at one o'clock, and assembled in the drawing room upstairs. We did not find the Grand Duchess in the room, seated in state, nor were we led up and presented to her, according to the English custom. The Russian mode was here followed, which, though it is very considerate to the feelings of those who for the first time find themselves in this novel position, entails much trouble, and demands some nerve and self posession, on the part of the great personage who holds the levée. This should seem to be the more so when that great personage is a young woman who has to confront a number of men, most of whom she has never seen in her life before, and who has to find something in conversation for all. We were arranged somehow, though I know not by whose suggestion – perhaps by that of Prince Gargarine, or that of Count Tolstoi, though I do not recollect them at the interview – in a sort of half moon or curve, stretching from the door, across the room to the window.
>
> The Grand Duchess entered the further end, by the door that communicates with the back drawing room, or whatever it might be, followed by the Countess Nesselrode. The Countess went over and stood by the window nearest the fireplace, sometimes looking out, and sometimes casting a glance and one ear towards what was going on during the interview. She was rather a portly lady in figure, at all events in comparison with her more delicate little Mistress.
>
> The Grand Duchess was younger and more slight in contour; her skin was fair, and if I remember rightly, not without freckles; but as freckles are an indication of a fine skin, they are not blemishes. She was a blonde in her hair, a tint that accorded well with her fair complexion. Her features were good, and if not thoroughly classical, they were pleasing. Lord Weymouth, who with Lady Weymouth, then lived in the Elysian Fields, North of the Vicarage, (at Rosebank Cottage, to the best of my recollection), stood on the right of the row of gentlemen, near the window, as being the visitor of the highest rank. The Grand Duchess, having momentarily glanced at us all, walked lightly up to Lord Weymouth, and held a conversation with him for several minutes. I think she talked to him in Italian, but to all the rest in English. And she took each one in succession, starting topics for all, and maintaining the subjects without difficulty, in admirable English. She was perfectly self-possessed, and equal to the occasion.

As she talked to other people, and I had leisure for observation, I remarked the movement of her throat as she talked, and it reminded me of the throat of a canary bird when it sings. What horrid creatures boys are! Some of them are not fit to be admitted into decent society. When she had noticed each in succession, she bowed, skipped back to her door, and vanished. The Countess Nesselrode followed her with a slower pace. Being thus left alone, we walked down stairs as we liked. She also, on another occasion, received the ladies of Sidmouth, but to this I was not witness.

There were several boat trips: the report of this one is particularly atmospheric:

SIDMOUTH   The Grand Duchess Helene on Monday embarked from this place in a steamer, which arrived the preceding day for her Imperial Highness's accommodation. The spectacle was of unrivalled interest. At twelve o'clock a temporary platform was prepared from the water's edge to the promenade, &c. covered with green baize; and the inhabitants and visitors, to the number of from 1,500 to 2,000, thronged to the beach in anticipation of their illustrious guest's arrival. The Russian and English colours, quartered on one flag, were hoisted in the Fort Field, and upwards of thirty pleasure boats stood off from the shore, many of them decorated with appropriate banners. At half-past two the officer of the coast-guard, Captain Mannikin, hailed the approach of her Imperial Highness; and one of the King's boats was rowed to the platform to convey the Grand Duchess and her cortege to the steamer, on boarding which the English and Russian standards were simultaneously hoisted on the foremast and stern respectively, and a brass band played airs suitable to the occasion. The gratification experienced from this lively and interesting scene every countenance bespoke, and a more auspicious day could not have occurred.
11 August, 1831   London Morning Post[15]

The Grand Duchess also visited Ladram Bay, Powderham Castle, and Bicton House, where she met Lord and Lady Rolle. Lady Rolle made several visits to Sidmouth to see the Grand Duchess at No 8 Fort Terrace, described in the newspapers as 'the Imperial Residence'.

Her time in Sidmouth was coming to an end. She was presented by John Wallis, proprietor of the Marine Library, with a leather-bound copy of pictures of the houses of Sidmouth, with a special new frontispiece of the Grand Duchess in the Fort Field, as shown opposite. Hutchinson describes her departure:

At seven o'clock in the morning of Wednesday the 24th of August 1831, Sidmouth was aroused by guns from the Preventive Station. This was a parting compliment to the Grand Duchess, who left this place on that day, having resided here exactly two months, namely from the 24th of June. She first proceeded to Cheltenham, and afterwards went to London and Windsor, where she visited Her Majesty Queen Victoria. [Here Hutchinson is guilty of a historical faux pas, as of course Victoria was not yet Queen.]

The three children stayed in Sidmouth with their governess until the Friday, before leaving to join their mother in Cheltenham, where the Grand Duchess took the waters and charmed the locals. She visited King William and Queen Adelaide at Windsor Castle on 7 October, and left Cheltenham for Hastings on 14 October before returning home.

THE GRAND DUCHESS AND PARTY AT THE FORTFIELD 1831

I would like to insert three post-scripts to this wonderful story.

Firstly, on a sad note, the baby Princess Alexandra, who had been left at home, died on 27 March the following year. Of the three little girls who played on the Fort Field, Marie, aged six in 1831, died when she was twenty-one, Elizabeth, aged five, died at the age of eighteen, and Catherine, who was four at the time of this visit lived to the comparatively old age of sixty-seven. The Grand Duchess was to have one more baby, Anne, who was born on 27 October, 1834 and died on 22 March, 1836.

Secondly, a last word from Peter Orlando Hutchinson:

> It may be remarked that as a memorial of her visit, the Russian two-necked Black Eagle displayed, was placed against the front of the house she had occupied, where it has remained ever since. It even continued there through the Russian War of 1854 and 1855, nobody thinking it necessary to take any notice of the circumstance. When I was a Lieutenant in the Volunteer Artillery, drilling in the Fort Field, I once or twice playfully pointed my carbine at it, but I never fired.

RUSSIAN EAGLE AT 7 and 8 FORTFIELD TERRACE 2006

Finally, from *The Sidmouth Observer and Visitors' List* of 28 September, 1892:

> Extract from 'The Gentlewoman' on the general decline of the Glen [the small valley next to the Fort Field]: ' Time was when Sidmouth was the resort of beauty and fashion, to which the mouldy-looking Imperial Eagle surmounting one of the cliff houses bears testimony. On inquiring its significance, one of the natives informed me with pardonable pride that a Russian Crown Princess, whose exact title she could not recall, had spent some weeks therein.' [16]

How quickly even the most sparkling of memories can fade...

CHAPTER SEVEN
ANOTHER FAMOUS RESIDENT

How do I love thee? Let me count the ways.
I love thee to the depth and breadth and height
My soul can reach, when feeling out of sight
For the ends of Being and ideal Grace.

From Sonnets from the Portuguese LXIII
Elizabeth Barrett Browning[1]

In 1832, just a year after the events in the previous chapter, another famous woman arrived at No 8 Fort Terrace: not royalty this time, but a poet.

❧ ELIZABETH BARRETT BROWNING ❧

Events four thousand miles away in the West Indies led indirectly to Fort Terrace being the home of Elizabeth Barrett. The campaign against slavery which had gathered momentum in Britain since the end of the eighteenth century, and led to the Abolition of the Slave Trade Act in 1807, was about to achieve its goal in the Abolition of Slavery Act in 1833 and the emancipation of slaves in the British Empire in 1834.

Elizabeth's father, Edward Moulton-Barrett, was of creole descent, generations of his family having owned sugar plantations in Jamaica. Interestingly, Elizabeth Barrett Browning is named in a list of 100 Great Black Britons: other famous 'B's in the list include Floella Benjamin (ex-children's TV presenter and now Chancellor of Exeter University) and Frank Bruno (former heavyweight boxer).[2] Financial problems relating to the plantations, and an insurrection of slaves and burning of plantations in December 1831, led the Barrett family to leave the family home of Hope End in Herefordshire. Elizabeth was the eldest of eleven children: their mother had died in 1828. So it was that in August 1832 she arrived with her Aunt Charlotte, her sisters and some of her brothers at Sidmouth, where her father had rented 8 Fort Terrace for 2 months. Their arrival was almost three weeks later than planned: their stay in Sidmouth was to be almost three years longer than planned.

The journey from Hope End was about one hundred and forty miles, which they did in two days, stopping overnight at Bath. Their arrival at the Terrace was not auspicious, as Elizabeth describes in a letter to Mrs Martin, a lifelong friend.[3]

> We arrived here almost in the dark, and were besieged by the crowd of disinterested tradespeople, who would attend us through the town to our house, to help to unload the carriages. This was not a particularly agreeable reception in spite of its cordiality; and the circumstance of there being not a human being in our house, and not even a rushlight burning, did not reassure us. People were tired of expecting us every day for three weeks.

Things soon picked up however and Elizabeth continued,

> We like very much what we have seen of it. The town is small and not superfluously clean, but, of course, the respectable houses are not a part of the town. Ours is one which the Grand Duchess Helena had, not at all grand, but extremely comfortable and cheerful, with a splendid sea view in front, and pleasant green hills and trees behind. The drawing-room's four windows all look to the sea, and I am never tired of looking out of them.

This letter concludes with a little botanical note:

> You may suppose what a southern climate this is, when I tell you that myrtles and verbena, three or four feet high, and hydrangeas are in flower in the gardens - even in ours, which is about a hundred and fifty yards from the sea. [Hydrangeas still flower in the garden of No 8.]

By the time she writes to Mrs Martin on 27 September, her father and two brothers have arrived, and she describes her father as being 'not only satisfied, but pleased with this place', and gives a glowing description of Sidmouth:

> It is scarcely possible, at least it seems so to me, to do otherwise than admire the beauty of the country. It is the very land of green lanes and pretty thatched cottages. I don't mean the kind of cottages which are generally thatched, with pigstyes and cabbages and dirty children, but thatched cottages with verandas and shrubberies, and sounds from the harp or piano coming through the windows.

In her letters, Elizabeth repeatedly refers to No 8 Fort Terrace as 'Rafarel House', this being presumed to be the name of the owner. Since the house was still in the ownership of the Manor Estate, it would more likely be the name of the leaseholder. This is interesting in that the house was still subject to the original 61 year lease of Elizabeth Spicer. It seems likely that at some stage following her son's horseback exploits on the cricket pitch at the end of the 1820s, the remainder of the lease was sold to the Rafarel family, members of which we know to have been living in Sidmouth at the time.

Since childhood Elizabeth had been in poor health, having had a chest complaint, and a back injury in her early teens. As for so many others, the Sidmouth air seems to have worked its magic on her.

Sidmouth: May 27,1833 My dearest Mrs. Martin, As for me, I have been quite well all the spring, and almost all the winter. I don't know when I have been so long well as I have been lately; without a cough or anything else disagreeable. Indeed, if I may place the influenza in a parenthesis, we have all been perfectly well, in spite of our fishing and boating and getting wet three times a day. There is good trout-fishing at the Otter, and the noble river Sid, which, if I liked to stand in it, might cover my ankles. And lately, Daisy and Sette and Occyta have studied the art of catching shrimps, and soak themselves up to their waists like professors. My love of water concentrates itself in the boat; and this I enjoy very much, when the sea is as blue and calm as the sky, which it has often been lately...Our plans are quite uncertain; and papa has not, I believe, made up his mind whether or not to take this house on after the beginning of next month, when our engagement with our present landlord closes.

The family did move to another house in Sidmouth at this point, possibly Norton Garth, just around the corner in what is now Station Road. This was not entirely satisfactory: in her letter to Mrs Martin of 7 September, 1833, Elizabeth writes:

We are still in the ruinous house. Without any poetical fiction, the walls are too frail for even me, who enjoy the situation in a most particularly particular manner, to have any desire to pass the winter within them. One wind we have had the privilege of hearing already; and down came the tiles while we were at dinner, and made us all think that down something else was coming. We have had one chimney pulled down to prevent it from tumbling down; and have received especial injunctions from the bricklayers not to lean too much out of the windows, for fear the walls should follow the destiny of the chimney... I have enjoyed its moonlight and its calmness all the summer; and am prepared to enjoy its tempestuousness of the winter with as true an enjoyment.

Fortunately, their stay in this house was only brief, and by November the family was living in Belle Vue, now called Cedar Shade, in All Saints Road. In a letter to Lady Margaret Cocks written from Belle Vue on 15 November, 1833 Elizabeth provides more detail:[4]

We have been twice on the very verge of leaving Sidmouth, from the difficulty of getting a house. In our first dilemma of this kind, we moved to one in a preparatory state to being a ruin... Altogether, to brave the winter there was out of the question. We should have been out of our senses to have thought of it—and Papa was so puzzled as to what other house would fit us, that he had all but resolved to carry us off to the Bristol Hot Wells. Now, without considering all my good reasons for wishing to stay at Sidmouth, I was rather in hot water about going to the Hot Wells. Yet if we had gone, I dare say I should have contrived to be happy; seeing that happiness lies more within than without—and the "depth saith, it is not in me"- A "moralitie", by the way, which did not lessen my pleasure at Papa's finding out at Sidmouth a pretty villa or rather cottage, with thatch and a viranda and a garden, and the viranda's due proportion of ivy & rose trees—about a quarter of a mile from the sea. The view of the sea is rather too indistinct to please me—we look at it over trees & the little town & the church steeple—but I am consoled by hearing it roaring, & by a genuine Devonshire lane with "hedgerow elms", bounding our garden. So here we are settled for at least six months!

And there they stayed for almost two years. What else do we know of Elizabeth's time in Sidmouth? She writes about some of the people she and her sisters met, and parties that her brothers went to with up to one hundred and sixty guests, but she herself was obviously not a 'party animal'. From a literary perspective, she published her translation of Aeschylus' *Prometheus Bound* in 1833, and wrote a few short poems.

She had a complex relationship with Hugh Boyd, a blind scholar. Boyd and his wife moved from Bath to Sidmouth to be near Elizabeth. This was a strange situation which was rather uncomfortable for all concerned, and culminated in the Boyd's moving away from Sidmouth before the end of May 1834, possibly because of Mrs Boyd's poor health. She died during the following autumn. During her time in Sidmouth, Elizabeth continued her involvement in Missionary and Bible Meetings. This led to another unusual relationship, this time with the minister of the Independent Chapel in that town, George Barrett Hunter (no relation). She developed a close friendship with him. He probably fell in love with her, but this was not reciprocated, though they remained friends long after he left the Chapel in February 1835. Both he and Boyd were 'unworldly, impractical, and idealistic, and both suffered from severe handicaps, mental or physical, which prevented them from earning an adequate living'.[5]

The Barretts left Sidmouth in the summer of 1835 for London. Elizabeth married Robert Browning against her father's wishes in 1846, and spent most of the rest of her life in Florence. She became England's most famous Victorian poetess. She was described as 'a woman of singular nobility and charm, and though not beautiful, [she] was remarkably attractive'. As a young woman she was 'a slight, delicate figure, with a shower of dark curls falling on each side of a most expressive face; large, tender eyes, richly fringed by dark eyelashes, and a smile like a sunbeam'. A rather less kind view of her by the Victorian novelist, Ann Thackeray Ritchie, described her as 'very small and brown with big, exotic eyes and an overgenerous mouth'.[6] Beauty, like history, is in the eye of the beholder.

ELIZABETH BARRETT BROWNING
by Field Talfourd
National Portrait Gallery

From the point of view of this history, perhaps we should remember her as someone who enjoyed living at Fort Terrace and who appreciated the seclusion and beauty of Sidmouth. On 22 September, 1834 she wrote to her friend, Miss Commeline:[7]

> We came to Sidmouth for two months, and you see we are here still; and when we are likely to go is as uncertain as ever. I like the place, and some of its inhabitants. I like the greenness and the tranquillity and the sea; and the solitude of one dear seat which hangs over it, and which is too far or too lonely for many others to like besides myself.
>
> We are living in a thatched cottage [Belle Vue], with a green lawn bounded by a Devonshire lane. Do you know what that is? Milton did when he wrote of 'hedgerow elms and hillocks green'. Indeed Sidmouth is a nest among elms; and the lulling of the sea and the shadow of the hills make it a peaceful one. But there are no majestic features in the country. It is all green and fresh and secluded; and the grandeur is concentrated upon the ocean without deigning to have anything to do with the earth. I often find my thoughts where my footsteps once used to be! but there is no use in speaking of that. . . .

A sense of shelter… I wonder if she ever met the Bishop of Llandaff when he came to visit his sisters.

✇   UNDER NEW OWNERSHIP   ✇

On 30 August, 1834, three weeks before Elizabeth Barrett wrote those words to her friend, an unusual event took place. After a period of 37 years, Fort Terrace acquired a new owner: or vice versa.

As we have seen, in 1797 Thomas Jenkins (the Younger) inherited the Manor of Sidmouth and therefore Fort Terrace, from his great uncle. We have no evidence that he took much interest in it, other than as a source of raising money to maintain his extravagant lifestyle. His wild dealings came to a head with a mortgage arrangement with his brother-in-law, Edward Hughes Ball Hughes in 1827. Jenkins borrowed £45,000 and put up the Manor of Sidmouth as security. Along with previous mortgages which Jenkins had made and which were taken into account by Hughes, this arrangement valued the Manor Estate at £65,000.

Subsequently, Jenkins struggled to keep up with his repayments. In 1832 we find that Hughes was already in possession of No 7 Fort Terrace, which he leased to Richard Farrant (Upholsterer) for seven years at £47 10s per annum. Things came to a head on 29 and 30 August, 1834 when a Decree of Foreclosure was issued in His Majesty's High Court of Chancery in which Edward Hughes Ball Hughes became the 'absolute owner irredeemable' of the Manor of Sidmouth, and the owner of Fort Terrace.[8]

Edward Hughes Ball was born in 1798, two years after Fort Terrace was 'completed'. Due to the death of an uncle on his mother's side, at the age of twenty-one he inherited an income of £40,000 per year, an enormous sum in those days. He changed his name to Edward Hughes Ball Hughes and lived an extravagant lifestyle, so much so that his friends called him 'Golden Ball'. He bought Oatlands House in Surrey after the death of the Duchess of York in 1820. He was to be seen at Oatlands shooting pheasants, dressed in the latest London fashion and followed by two gamekeepers carrying his guns, or driving around the London parks in his chocolate coloured coach drawn by four white horses and with two liveried grooms. He was a compulsive and prodigious gambler: in one twenty-four hour session, he and four friends lost £100,000.[9]

'THE GOLDEN BALL'
(EDWARD HUGHES BALL HUGHES)
by Richard Dighton
National Portrait Gallery, London

He was handsome and charming, but not particularly successful in long-term relationships. However, in 1822, as the cigarette card showed on page 19, he married Marina Mercandotti, a fifteen year old Spanish dancer, in the face of stiff competition from other dandies of the time. This was the subject of much amusement, resulting in a cartoon commemorating the event, the original of which is in Sidmouth Museum.

THE WEDDING BALL *by J Fairburn*   Sidmouth Museum

The point of this cartoon was that Miss Mercandotti was the protégée of Lord Fife: rumour had it that he was her father, hence the Scotsman playing a fife, and the reference to the Highland Fling. Perhaps the tabloid press *has* softened a little over the years.

The Devon Record Office holds the decree of divorce between Edward Hughes Ball Hughes and Marina Mercandotti in 1839, based on the grounds of *her* adultery.

It is unlikely that he spent much time in Sidmouth, as London, Bath and Brighton were the places to be and to be seen. His impact on Sidmouth was more due to his absence than his presence, as we shall see.

His lavish lifestyle led to decline, and he retired to Paris, apparently to escape his creditors. Fortunately for him, he managed to sell Oatlands for a high price, which enabled him to continue to live in comparative luxury until his death in 1862.

❧ LAST OF THE HANOVERIANS ❦

The death of William IV on 20 June, 1837, and the beginning of Queen Victoria's reign, marked the end of the 123-year association of the British monarchy with that of Hanover, as constitutionally a woman could not rule Hanover. It also heralded a tide of unprecedented and far-reaching change on a world-wide scale.

A few years earlier, in October 1831, just after the visit to Fortfield Terrace of the Grand Duchess Helena and before that of Elizabeth Barrett Browning, the Rev Sydney Smith, speaking at Taunton, compared the Lords' opposition to change, by rejection of the English Reform Bill, to the efforts of Dame Partington. The story goes that Mrs Partington had a cottage down by the sea in Sidmouth. In the severe storm of November 1824, in which the Chit Rock was washed away, the gale drove the sea into her cottage. Her attempts to repel the water with her mop failed, and she had to retreat upstairs. In the words of Rev Smith:

> *The Atlantic was roused; Mrs. Partington's spirit was up. But I need not tell you that the contest was unequal; the Atlantic Ocean beat Mrs. Partington. She was excellent at a slop or puddle, but should never have meddled with a tempest.*[10]

In the first forty-seven years of the history of Fortfield Terrace we have come a long way, from Rome to Sidmouth, from Georgian times to Victorian. We shall now go on to look at the ways in which Sidmouth and Fortfield Terrace coped with enormous social change during the Victorian Era, and how the lives of the people who stayed or lived here adapted to those changing times. It may be that Mrs Partington's legacy, either willingly or by default, lived on.

CHAPTER EIGHT
COLLECTING VICTORIANA

Having survived the errant catapulted stone when she was a baby in Sidmouth, Victoria was crowned Queen on 28 June, 1838, just five weeks after her eighteenth birthday. She was to become the longest reigning British monarch, ruling over the most powerful industrial nation in the world. She presided over a period of unprecedented change that affected not only people's world view, but also the way in which they lived.

Although there is no evidence that she was wheeled along Fort Terrace in her pram, this does seem quite likely, and the lack of evidence has never deterred the opportunists, as in this advertisement for the Eagle Restaurant, Nos 7 and 8 Fortfield Terrace, from 1947.

Eagle House & Restaurant, Sidmouth

This imposing 18th Century Georgian residence stands in Fortfield Terrace directly facing the Cricket Ground and Sea. Many notable personages have entered its doors, including QUEEN VICTORIA, THE EMPRESS EUGENIE AND ELIZABETH BARRETT BROWNING. THE GRAND DUCHESS HELENE OF RUSSIA stayed here in 1831 and residents of Sidmouth paid her a compliment by setting the Russian Eagle over the house, where it still remains. The interior has been completely converted without affecting its dignity or charm, and now contains residential suites and a first-class restaurant, where one can obtain good food, excellently cooked, and served amid delightful surroundings.

EAGLE RESTAURANT
FORTFIELD TERRACE
SIDMOUTH

Morning Coffee - Luncheons - Afternoon Tea
English Cuisine

OPEN ON SUNDAYS

Personally supervised by the Proprietors
Make the 'Eagle' a rendezvous during your stay in Sidmouth
Tables may be reserved by Telephoning 845

from OFFICIAL GUIDE & SOUVENIR OF SIDMOUTH 1947
West Country Studies Library, Exeter

DEVELOPMENTAL DELAY

The growth of the middle classes and the ability of more people to take seaside holidays, coupled with the improvement of public transport, notably the railway, had a profound effect on the development of seaside towns like Sidmouth.

Though a source of frustration at the time, the late arrival of the railway in Sidmouth, not until 1874, was an important factor in protecting Sidmouth from the excesses of development suffered by some other seaside towns.

The other major factor that helped to protect Sidmouth was that until John Balfour became Lord of Sidmouth Manor in 1869, a succession of uninterested absentee landlords left the Manor Estate, which included a large part of the town, in a state of disrepair, which was certainly perceived at the time as hindering Sidmouth's development.

Lethaby's Sidmouth Journal and Directory of 1 March, 1864 carried an editorial which summed up the feeling in the town:

> *Sidmouth is the most beautiful watering place on the south coast of Devon… But she needs many essential improvements in order to bring her up to the level of modern taste and requirements. This is obvious to all who, having visited other seaside resorts, have made a visit to Sidmouth.*[1]

Townspeople were urged to 'be up and doing' if they desired to 'partake of that prosperity which must follow on the opening of the railway'. The editorial continued:

> *The great 'Man of the Mountain', under which Sidmouth has long groaned, is the Manor property. The enfranchisement of this property, and its distribution among a few wealthy and spirited individuals, would be one of the greatest improvements which we have in view. A fine, large, handsome hotel, with a terrace of magnificent lodging houses, and a tasteful and economically fitted up hot and cold bathing establishment, all in the modern style, and somewhere on the Esplanade, with an accommodation jetty opposite for promenade, and for facilitating the disembarkation and embarkation of pleasure parties, is another essential improvement, which we desire to see carried out.*

Looking back, perhaps we should be grateful that circumstances conspired to maintain the essential beauty of Sidmouth through those changing times.

COLLECTING BITS AND PIECES

The Victorian obsessions with collecting and with detail mean that a lot of very useful and interesting data were recorded, which are the basis of the rest of this book. For the purposes of this history there are six main sources of information.

For most of the period in question the local newspapers published 'Visitors' Lists'. This was a voluntary scheme whereby lodging-house keepers and other responsible individuals notified the newspaper about who was staying in their property each week. The lists had to be submitted by each Tuesday evening. This system enabled those visitors who wished to do so to announce their arrival in town, and was probably a good way of ensuring that, as is the way in small communities, locals had a fair idea of everybody else's business. As a result, there is a record of everyone who was recorded as staying in Fortfield Terrace from 1849 to 1901, with a few small gaps.

While this gives a fairly complete and continuous record, it is only a list of names, with no detail. Sometimes the names themselves are informative. For instance, we know that for a fortnight in April 1891 'the Right Rev the Lord Bishop of Winchester and the Misses Thorold' stayed at No 2, and for a fortnight in March 1893 'Professor and Mrs Darwin and family from Cambridge', Charles Darwin's son and family, stayed at No 10.

Most of the names appearing in these lists are of less widely recognisable people, though all in their own way are interesting. Clergymen, doctors, artists, clerical workers and business people all come and go, and as the century progresses the individual clientele becomes less identifiable as more and more people are able to take a seaside holiday. Some residents stay for a week, others for several years. Some come back year after year, just as they do now. In the main, we can only guess at what they were like, and assume that they enjoyed life in the Terrace.

CENSUS RETURNS

The first detailed census was taken in 1841, and all of the 10-yearly national censuses up to 1911 have now been made available to the public. While the Visitors' Lists give a continuous but limited view of the inhabitants of Fortfield Terrace, the censuses give a much more detailed but discontinuous snapshot once every ten years. These isolated moments in time tell another story, one which includes the working people for whom Fortfield Terrace was not a holiday home: the lodging-house keepers, cooks, maids and housekeepers who kept the whole enterprise running. By virtue of the fact that this was a compulsory record, it trapped and preserved for all time the names of anyone, regardless of social status, at a given address on census night.

So, for example, while *The Sidmouth Observer and Visitors' List* records the stay of the Bishop of Winchester in 1891, because he was there on census night, the Census gives us more of an insight into who was at No 2 with him, and the social structure of the household. The census entry for No 2 on 5 April, 1891 lists the following occupants of Mrs Fitzgerald's Lodging House:

No 2 FORTFIELD TERRACE			AGE	STATUS	BIRTHPLACE
Mary Fitzgerald	Head	Widow	52	Lodging House Keeper	Sidmouth
Mary A Fitzgerald	Daughter	Single	22	Help Domestic	Sidmouth
Thomas E Fitzgerald	Son		13	Scholar	Sidmouth
Emily Thomas	Servant	Single	19	General Servant	Colyton
Anthony Thorold	Head	Widower	65	Bishop of Winchester	Haigham, Lincs
Dorothy M Thorold	Daughter	Single	18		St Pancras
Sybil E Thorold	Daughter	Single	16		St Pancras
Agnes F A Ricoffi	Servant	Single	63	Governess	Wurtemburg
George Clark	Servant	Single	28	Butler	Stratford on Avon
Margaret Taylor	Lodger	Single	43	Living on means	Cupar, Fife
Graham F Ross	Nephew		12		Glasgow
Barbara A Pesel	Visitor	Widow	43	Living on means	South Australia
Florence Pesel	Visitor	Single	21	Living on means	Huddersfield

The Rt Rev Anthony Thorold was there with his two teenage daughters, their governess (incidentally from the childhood home town of Grand Duchess Helena) and his butler. A search of further sources reveals the sad story behind this. He was widowed twice: his second wife, Emily, died in 1877, when Sybil was only two years old.

The census returns also document the changing clientele, and the way in which holidays were taken. At the beginning of the Victorian period, visitors would have rented a whole house and brought their own staff with them, cooks, maids and butlers. As time went by, the trend was for the properties to become lodging-houses, with a resident lodging-house keeper (usually female) and staff. It was not until 1877 that some houses in Fortfield Terrace were actually called 'lodging-houses'. Gradually, with the exception of No 8, the whole Terrace became lodging-houses. As Walton points out, 'The seaside provided respectable employment for large numbers of spinsters and widows who needed the income from lodging-house keeping to make ends meet.'[2]

Census returns also give us an insight into life for ordinary people during these times, in some ways quite familiar to us today. So, for example, the 1891 census shows the following family group at No 7, with a good old Sidmouth name, still part of the present-day town:

No 7 FORTFIELD TERRACE			AGE	STATUS	BIRTHPLACE
Allan Pile	Head	Married	34	Gardener	Sidmouth
Alice Pile	Wife	Married	28	Lodging House Keeper	Bromham, Wilts
Arthur J Pile	Son		7	Scholar	Sidmouth
Allan C Pile	Son		5	Scholar	Sidmouth
Alice Pile	Daughter		1m		Sidmouth
Ann Davis	Mother in Law	Married	60	Nurse domestic	Bromham, Wilts
Susan Banfield	Servant	Single	22	General Servant	Sidbury

Alice Pile, the lodging-house keeper, has just had her third baby, and her mother Ann, has come down from Bromham (near Devizes in Wiltshire) to help. With three small children and his mother-in-law in the house, gardening may have seemed an attractive escape for Allan.

LOCAL NEWSPAPERS AND JOURNALS

Sidmouth Museum contains a collection of local newspapers and journals of the period. The main ones are *HARVEY'S SIDMOUTH DIRECTORY and general advertiser for Sidmouth and the neighbourhood* (1849-1853), *LETHABY'S SIDMOUTH JOURNAL AND DIRECTORY* (1862-1888), *THE SIDMOUTH DIRECTORY AND GENERAL ADVERTISER* (1868-1887) and *THE SIDMOUTH OBSERVER AND VISITORS' LIST* (1891-1901). They contain huge amounts of useful information about events and people, as well as the Visitors' Lists.

We often find out more about people in a short time after their death than we do in the years when they are with us.

So we find from the Visitors' List that from 1 July, 1869 to 1 May, 1870, Mr and Mrs Lowrie and family were living at No 2 Fortfield Terrace. It is not until *Lethaby's Journal* of 1 November, 1874 that we find out a little more detail.

> *DEPARTED FRIENDS – Many of our readers will recollect Mr and Mrs Lowrie, who with their two daughters resided several years at Belmont, and subsequently on Fortfield Terrace… Mrs Lowrie was an invalid, and the affectionate husband was often to be seen helping to wheel her along in an easy chair. Mr Ebenezer Lowrie died on May 30, 1874.* [3]

The Visitors' List of December 1869 shows simply that a Mr and Miss Campion stayed with Mr Butcher at No 9 for two weeks. A year later *Lethaby's* reports:

> *In August last a gentleman died in Sidmouth, who had resided here a few months with his afflicted daughter. They had also been lodging here in 1869. Mr Campion was a remarkably quiet, unobtrusive gentleman, and but few persons in the town had any inkling of his great wealth. The young lady, his daughter (Mary), will be remembered by many in Sidmouth, from a peculiarity in her manner, and her always having a confidential attendant with her.*[4]

And on 10 June, 1914 the *Sidmouth Chronicle* by John Tindall reports the death of Mr Allan J Pile of Fortfield Terrace, age 57, who in 1891 was celebrating the birth of his daughter at No 7. He had been on the committee of Sidmouth Horticultural Society for 20 years and a bell-ringer for 31 years.[5]

The newspapers and journals also keep us informed of events and people connected with the Terrace over the years, giving us a flavour of life in Fortfield Terrace in Victorian times.

LOCAL AND NATIONAL ARCHIVES

County Record Offices are a valuable source of information, containing documents ranging from legal documents to personal letters, all available to the public. So, for example, deeds kept at Devon Record Office document the early occupancy of Fortfield Terrace. The West Country Studies Library also contains useful books and documents including *Trewman's Exeter Flying Post* going back to the eighteenth century.

Sometimes one has to go further afield: to the Shropshire Record Office for the will of Mary Floyd, or Bristol Record Office for the letters of Edmund Butcher. These records are fascinating, but sometimes require patience and good eyesight. For example, this is a letter from Edmund Butcher to his mother in the 1820s. They certainly knew about saving paper and postage in those days.

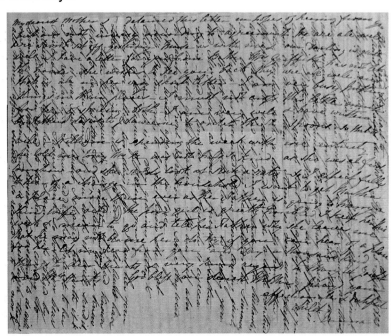

**LETTER FROM
EDMUND BUTCHER
TO HIS MOTHER
c.1820**
Bristol Record Office

The Internet allows one to gather information which would have been virtually inaccessible without it. So, for example, it is possible to search the Records Offices to see whether they hold relevant documents, using the Access To Archives website, or to search worldwide for names, places and events. An Internet search discovered the letters from Edward Copleston to his sisters in Fort Terrace in a collection at Yale University, USA. The availability of census records online makes extensive searching of these a practical possibility.

PEOPLE

There is a sixth source of information, which becomes more important as we explore more recent history: that is, talking to people. Though we will no longer come across first-hand verbal accounts of the Victorian period, there are many people who can recount stories of those times told by the previous generation. And on the whole, it is the lives of people in that generation that this part of the story is all about. So, for example, shortly before his death, I was able to talk to Brian Fitzgerald, grandson of the above-mentioned Mrs Fitzgerald, lodging-house keeper of No 2 Fortfield Terrace. I hope that this initial account will stimulate a telling of many other stories which will become part of an ongoing and developing history.

❧ DISPLAYING THE COLLECTION ❦

I intend to present our collection of Terrace Victoriana a decade at a time, with some reference to the historical context in which lives were lived and events unfolded. People at that time were curious and becoming well-informed about what was happening in the Empire and the world in general.

THE READING ROOM, SIDMOUTH 1876
by Col. Hawker Sidmouth Museum

Then, as now, they had opinions about most things.

MRS HAWKER
by Col. Hawker Sidmouth Museum

Most were in agreement that whatever was happening in the outside world, Sidmouth was, on the whole, a very good and comfortable place in which to live.

CHAPTER NINE
1837 - 1849

☙   **BRAVE NEW WORLD**   ❧

1837 - 1849

In **1837**, at the age of eighteen, Victoria ascended the throne of what was to become one of the most powerful empires in history, and Charles Dickens wrote *Oliver Twist*. **1838** was the year of full emancipation of British West Indian slaves, the culmination of events which led indirectly not only to Elizabeth Barrett Browning coming to live at Fortfield Terrace, but also to the migration of my ancestors from China to British Guiana, either as indentured labourers to work in the sugar-cane fields or in associated occupations. **1839** saw British troops capturing Kabul, in a move eerily evocative of the events of 2001.

In **1840**, the year that Victoria and Albert were married, New Zealand was annexed to Britain in the Treaty of Waitangi and Dickens wrote *Nicholas Nickleby*. In **1841** Dickens wrote *The Old Curiosity Shop* and in **1842** China ceded Hong Kong to Britain 'in perpetuity'. The same year, in Britain, the employment of women, girls and boys under the age of ten in mines was made illegal. **1843** saw the Empire expanding in Africa to include Gambia, Natal and Basutoland, and Dickens wrote *Martin Chuzzlewit* and *A Christmas Carol*.

In the midst of increasing prosperity, the potato famine in Ireland and Scotland began in **1845** with devastating effects. **1847** was a good year for female authors, with the publication of *Jane Eyre*, *Wuthering Heights* and *Agnes Grey* by the Bronte sisters. The fact that this was a good year for female authors was not generally realised until the following year when a London publisher was shocked to find that the author of his best-selling novel, *Jane Eyre*, was a woman. That year, **1848** saw revolutions in Russia, France, the Austrian Empire and Prussia, Dickens wrote *Dombey and Son*, and Marx and Engels wrote the *Communist Manifesto*. The decade came to an end with the Punjab being annexed to British rule and Dickens writing *David Copperfield* in **1849**.

QUEEN VICTORIA AS A GIRL *by Richard Westhall*
The Royal Collection

ಶಿ MEANWHILE, BACK IN SIDMOUTH ಹಿ

Prosperity at home and overseas was reflected in the development of seaside towns like Sidmouth. In his 1838 guide, *The Beauties of the Shore*, D McNee Stirling wrote:

> *The seats, mansions and villas, of the resident gentry, add vastly to the charms of Sidmouth. They are the gems of the vale, and from every point of its superabounding eminences, the eye rests with delight on the uniform beauty of their construction, and the sweetly discriminated outlines of the elegantly laid-out grounds, by which they are generally encompassed.*[1]

This picture from *Rock's Royal Cabinet Album,* probably from a few years later, illustrates, rather beautifully, this view of the valley.

SIDMOUTH FROM SALCOMBE HILL Rock's Royal Cabinet Album

But in the Brave New World, places like Sidmouth were to become the destination for a much more broadly based population.

> *During the 1830s and 40s the balance of patronage generally tipped towards the seaside… The seaside resorts were better able to tap the rapidly expanding sources of demand among the emergent middle classes. During this period too the seaside began to compete increasingly effectively with the spas not only for the mainly pleasure-seeking visitors of high summer, but also as places of winter retreat and regular residence for wealthy invalids.*[2]

Sidmouth's development as a cultural centre was highlighted by a concert at the London Hotel on Saturday, 22 August, 1840, with Franz Liszt, the great Hungarian pianist, topping the bill. He was, as we have seen, a great favourite of Grand Duchess Helena. Liszt said of Sidmouth:

> *The countryside that we have been through is most delightful, Sidmouth seems particularly beautiful and everywhere there are wonderful parks.*[3]

No doubt this concert would have been very much in the spirit of the Sid Vale Association, which was founded in 1846 as the Sidmouth Improvement Committee. It is the oldest civic society in Britain, and it continues today, vigorously pursuing its aims to 'protect the beauties and amenities of the neighbourhood and to promote and aid its cultural development'.

❧ PORTRAIT OF A LADY ❧

Unfortunately, this period is not documented in local journals. Even Peter Orlando Hutchinson has surprisingly little to say. He was not, however, idle, and recalls this rather whimsical episode. Earlier in this book we saw portraits of Thomas Jenkins, Lord of Sidmouth Manor and commissioner of Fortfield Terrace, and of Michael Novosielski, the architect of Fortfield Terrace. These were painted in the late eighteenth century by Angelica Kauffmann (1741-1807), a celebrated artist of the time, who at that stage was living in Rome.

SELF PORTRAIT
between 1780 and 1785
by Angelica Kauffmann
The State Hermitage Museum
St Petersburg

Hutchinson recalls:

> *It may have been about the year 1848 that a lady in Sidmouth told me there was a painting in a cottage in Sidbury, reputed to have been done by Angelica Kauffmann, and that it was probably part of the acquirements of Jenkins, and that it may once have belonged to his nephew Joseph Jenkins, when Joseph resided at Cotford near Sidbury. Upon hearing this, I walked out and made enquiry, and at last found the object of my search in a house opposite the west end of the church. The first glance however was enough. What I saw had never been done by Angelica Kauffmann. It was a miserable coarse daub of a female half-length, apparently done by some village sign painter in England… I returned to Sidmouth satisfied.* [4]

Presumably the painting he saw looked nothing like the one above. Hutchinson obviously did not consider this a wasted journey: the walk from Sidmouth to Sidbury has always been a pleasant one.

❧ LIFE IN THE TERRACE ❧

Sometime between 1841 and 1849, No 1 Fort Terrace, as the Terrace was then called, was divided into Nos 1 and 1½. The internal layout meant that the division produced some interesting anomalies now reflected in 'flying freehold'.

The 1841 census tells us who was living in Fort Terrace on June 6 that year. The following were at Nos 1-7:

1	Frances Copplestone	60	Independent
	Caroline Copplestone	50	Independent
	Catherine Hoskins	30	Servant
	Rhoda Millen	16	Servant
2	No entry		
3	Anna Schimmelpenninck	60	
	Priscilla Strudwick	25	Servant
	Mary Brown	30	Servant
4	No entry		
5	Martha White	60	
	Mary Fry	65	
	Martha Head	30	
	Sarah Fry	25	
	Elizabeth Smale	30	
	Mary Small	30	
6	Thomas Eton	75	
	Frances Eton	35	
	Mary Dore	35	
	Emma Tannersby	20	
7	Dowager Lady Audley	70	
	Elizabeth Maidment	35	
	Mary Day	20	
	Mary Harris	45	
	Elizabeth Harris	15	
	Wilhelmina Pratt	55	
	Stella Goodwin	15	
	Jane Ebdon	30	
	Charles Croyden	30	
	Ann House	20	

We have already met in chapter 5 the Misses Copleston at No 1, and Miss Schimmelpenninck at No 3. In 1820, Captain White RN was living at No 5. In this census, his wife Martha is there on her own. It may be that Captain (by then Rear-Admiral) White was away on active service or more likely that he had died.

❧ A CASE OF MISTAKEN IDENTITY ❧

Dowager Lady Audley appears in the 1841 census living at No 7 with her household. She was Augusta Henrietta Catherine Audley, widow of the 19th Lord Audley of Heleigh in Staffordshire. Her age is recorded as 70, but in fact she would have been 79. Even censuses cannot compel a Lady to divulge her true age!

Her death is reported in *The Annual Register* (edited by Edmund Burke) of 1844:

> *Died April 1844 at her residence at Sidmouth, age 82, the Right Hon. Anne Jane, Dowager Lady Audley. She was the eldest daughter of the late Vice-Admiral Sir Ross Donnelly, K.C.B., was married in 1816, and left widow in 1837, having had issue the present Lord Audley, three other sons and two daughters.[5]*

Unfortunately, the only accurate statements in this obituary are, ironically, her age and her place of death. The rest of the information mistakenly refers to the Dowager Lady Jane Audley who was happily alive and well, and died eleven years later. The confusion arose because of the unlikely event of having two Dowager Lady Audleys living in Sidmouth. Augusta was the second wife of George Thicknesse-Touchet, 19th Lord Audley of Heleigh in Staffordshire and step-mother of George Thicknesse-Touchet, 20th Lord Audley of Heleigh, who married Anne as stated in 1816. Augusta was therefore Anne's step-mother-in-law. She had been a widow since 1818 and presumably moved to Sidmouth to live with her family at Audley Cottage (now Audley, in All Saints Road). Her step-son George died in 1837, following which Anne left Sidmouth and Augusta moved to Fort Terrace. We do not know how long she stayed at No 7 Fort Terrace, but it is quite possible that she spent her last years there.

More straightforwardly, No 10 was unoccupied, and Nos 8 and 9 were occupied by:

8	Ann Hamstead	35	
	Elizabeth Hamstead	9	
	Frances Hamstead	7	
	Ann Hamstead	5	
	Mary Newton	30	
	Laura Hood	28	
	Elizabeth Wheaton	16	
	Frances Greaves	50	Independent
9	Mark Moggridge	55	Independent Minister
	Theodore Moggridge	30	Physician
	Sarah Moggridge	21	
	Hermione Tozer	20	
	Ann Bale	25	

Theodore Mogridge, at No 9, was a Member of the Royal College of Surgeons and the author of *A Descriptive Sketch Of Sidmouth comprising its ancient and modern history.* He and his father Mark, the Independent Church Minister, moved to Arcot House where Mark died in 1846.

The first Visitors' List appears in Harvey's Sidmouth Directory at the beginning of 1849. It lists the following people staying in Fort Terrace at the time.

Nos.	1	1 1/2	2	3	4	5	6	7	8	9	10
03/01/1849	Mrs Hopkins	the Misses Copleston				Mrs Admiral White	Capt (RN) and Mrs Fulford and family	the Misses Kennet Dawson (a)	Mr Mrs and Miss Dennis	Capt and Mrs Brown and family	Mrs Bennett and family

❧ THE FULFORDS ❧

The Fulford family of Dunsford is an old Devon family. Benjamin Wete Fulford married Joanna-Gerrard Galpin (born 1754). Their eldest son Colonel Baldwin Fulford (1775 – 1847) was Lieutenant-Colonel to the East Devon Militia. He succeeded to the family estate after the death of his uncle, John Fulford, in 1780. Interestingly, the Fulford Family also owned the patronage of the Parish of Offwell, and D M Stirling records that John sold this to the Rev J B Copplestone's (sic) father.

As we saw in Chapter Two, Joanna-Gerrard Fulford, by then widowed, became the first leaseholder of No 6 Fort Terrace in 1795, the tenancy being for two lives, to be continued by her daughters Elizabeth Mary (born c.1775) and Florence Ann (born c.1780). We know that Joanna and Florence were living at No 6 Fort Terrace in 1813 and Joanna in 1820.

In the census of 1841, Florence Ann Fulford, 62 and unmarried, was living with her nephew Baldwin (II) (age 37) and his mother, Anna Maria, at 3 Louisa Terrace, Exmouth. By 1851 she was back at Great Fulford, Dunsford, with Baldwin, Anna-Maria age 70, and two of his sisters, Louisa and Philippa (both 29).

The Gentleman's Magazine records in its 1839 obituaries, a death on July 5: 'At Sidmouth, Elizabeth Florence, second daughter of B Fulford Esq of Great Fulford'. It is likely that this was Elizabeth Mary. There is no reference to a married name or to where in Sidmouth she was living.

From 1849 to 1853 Captain John Fulford and his family lived at No 6 Fort Terrace. John was the grandson of Joanna. He was born on 16 February, 1809. He entered Royal Naval College in 1821, and rose through the ranks.

From 1845 he was Commander (second-in-charge) of *President*, flagship, Cape of Good Hope, commanded by William Pearse Stanley. From 1854 he was Captain of *Conway*, flagship of Rear-Admiral William Fairbrother Carroll, Queenstown. From 1856 he was Captain of *Hogue*, flagship of Rear-Admiral Henry Ducie Chads, Queenstown. He then left southern Africa, and from 1857 he was Captain of *Ganges*, flagship of Rear-Admiral Robert Lambert Baynes, Pacific Fleet.

John had a harbour named after him on Saltspring Island, just off the east coast of Vancouver Island, British Columbia, and in 1866 he became a Rear-Admiral.

He married Isabella Russell of South Bank, near Edinburgh, some time between 1840 and 1846. They had three children, Cecil (born 1846), Louisa (born 1849) and Reginald Baldwin (born 1851). Both Louisa and Reginald were born at No 6 Fort Terrace. During the time of his residence in Sidmouth, Captain Fulford was between commissions. By 1871, John and his wife Isabella were living with their daughter Louisa Maria in Bemerton, Wiltshire, and they were still there in 1881, John being described in the 1881 census as a 'Retired Admiral'.

John's older brother, Francis, was born in Sidmouth in 1803, probably at No 6. He went on to become the first Anglican Bishop of Montreal, Canada, and founder of the Art Association of Montreal.

❧ BRAVE OLD WORLD ❧

Devon Record Office holds the will of William Spicer of Courtlands, Withycombe Rawleigh, Devonshire dated August 1, 1844. He was the son of Elizabeth Spicer, the original leaseholder of No 8, and the same Mr Spicer who in the 1830s boldly rode his horse on the Fortfield during a cricket match to assert his rights as tenant.

CHAPTER TEN
1850 - 1859

❧ MORE OF THE SAME ❧

1850 - 1859

The second half of the nineteenth century began much as the first had ended for Britain, with some notable creative endeavours and a touch of imperial aggression. In **1850** Elizabeth Barrett Browning, best known for her description of the hydrangeas in the garden at No 8 Fortfield Terrace, wrote her second-best-known work, *Sonnets from the Portuguese*. **1851** was the year of the Great Exhibition in the Crystal Palace and in **1852** Britain annexed Burma. In **1854** Britain and France declared war against Russia to begin the Crimean War, including the infamous Charge of the Light Brigade at Balaclava. The following year, Florence Nightingale was dubbed 'the lady with the lamp' for her nursing of wounded soldiers in the Crimea. As we have already seen, our Grand Duchess Helena of Russia was doing the same, a few miles away behind enemy lines: a far cry from a peaceful summer spent in Sidmouth, where her eagle still looked out over the Fort Field.

In **1855**, a world away in another continent, David Livingstone 'discovered' the Victoria Falls. The Treaty of Paris in **1856** brought the Crimean War to an end. In **1857** Elizabeth Barrett Browning wrote *Aurora Leigh* and, presumably at a loose end after the conclusion of the Russian conflict, Britain and France declared war on China. Technology was marching on and in **1858** the recently laid transatlantic telegraph cable broke down. 'Big Ben' was installed in the clock tower of the Houses of Parliament, and India was 'transferred' from the East India Company to the British Crown. **1859** saw the publication of *On The Origin Of Species* by Charles Darwin, bringing the decade to a thoughtful if controversial end.

In 1850, Fort Terrace was first referred to as Fortfield Terrace, as it has been ever since. Communications were moving on and in October that year the Royal Mail introduced a new four-horse mail service from Sidmouth to Exeter via Ottery St Mary. This ran four times a day and was designed to connect with the mail trains running to and from London.

The Gentleman's Magazine reported the death on 27 June, 1850 of Mrs White, widow of Rear-Admiral George White at Sidmouth, ending that family's thirty-three year occupancy of No 5 Fortfield Terrace.

The census of March 30, 1851 recorded the following occupants of Fortfield Terrace:

1	Mrs Hopkins	Head	Absent			
	Kathrine Cockell	Visitor (niece)	Single	20	Clergyman's Daughter	Upton Scudamore, Wilts
	Jane Teed	Servant	Single	29	Lady's Maid	Sidbury
	Sarah Mellish	Servant	Widow	40	Cook	Heavitree
1 1/2	Frances Copplestone	Head	Single	70	Annuitant	Offwell
	Caroline Copplestone	Sister	Single	60	Annuitant	Offwel
	Mary Ann Hutchings	Servant	Single	26	House Maid	Northleigh
	Susan Greenslade	Servant	Single	25	Cook	Offwell
	Mary Ann Palmer	Servant	Single	22	Lady's Maid	Taunton
4	Gustavius Smith	Head	Married	59	Devon Magistrate	Newington Butts Middlesex
	Jane Smith	Wife	Married	60		Middlesex
	Hannah Travers	Visitor	Single	57	Fund Holder	Middlesex
	Elizabeth Helman	Servant	Widow	38	Cook	Kentisbeare
	Elizabeth Slade	Servant	Single	20	House Maid	Sidmouth
6	John Fulford	Head	Married	42	Capt RN (Half-Pay)	Dunsford
	Isabella Fulford	Wife	Married	35		Scotland
	Cecil W R Fulford	Son	Single	5	Scholar	St Leonards on sea
	Louisa Maria Fulford	Daughter	Single	1		Sidmouth
	Reginald Baldwin Fulford	Son	Single	1m		Sidmouth
	Mary A Jane	Servant	Single	24	Nurse	Barnstaple
	Celina Bowyer	Servant	Single	21	House Maid	Chardstock
	May Oades	Servant	Single	19	Cook	Tedburn St Mary
	Ann Smale	Servant	Single	16	Under Nurse	Chawley
7	Frances Mary Kennet Dawson	Head	Single	56	Fund Holder	Wakefield, Yorks
	Jane Kennet Dawson	Sister	Single	41	Fund Holder	Sandal Magna
	Jane Stokes	Servant	Single	28	Cook	Ottery St Mary
	Susan Quirk	Servant	Single	20	House Maid	Sidmouth
8	William Toller	Head	Married	45	Fund Holder	Barnstaple
	Elizabeth Toller	Wife	Married	32		Sidmouth
	Caroline Toller	Daughter	Single	7	Scholar	Instow
	Ellen Toller	Daughter	Single	6	Scholar	born At Sea
	William Taprell	Visitor	Married	50	Barrister	Barnstaple
	Ellen Taprell	Visitor	Married	41		Bristol
	Harriet Weaton	Servant	Single	28	Lady's Maid	Farnham
	Susan Hebditch	Servant	Single	23	House Maid	Yeovil
	William Levermore	Servant	Single	17	Footman	Broadway
	Mary Trickey	Servant	Married	43	Cook	Child St Lawrence
9	Edmund Butcher	Head	Married	59	Retired from Sugar Trade	Middlesex
	Sarah Butcher	Wife	Married	54		Bristol
	Edward Lyde Butcher	Son	Single	23	Artist in Painting and Drawing	Bristol
	Charles H Butcher	Son	Single	18	Classical Teaching	Bristol
	Elizabeth Russell	Servant	Single	38	General Servant	Northleigh

Nos 2, 3, 5 and 10 were unoccupied. Among the usual suspects we find Gustavius Smith and his wife living at No 4. They arrived at No 4 Fortfield Terrace in February 1851 and were there until at least the end of 1853. As the census states, he was a Devon Magistrate. In his book *The Beauties of the Shore*,[1] D McNee Stirling records that he sat as a magistrate at the monthly petty sessions at Honiton, with the Rev J G Copleston and Sir John Kennaway, amongst others. The Records of the Devon Quarter Sessions of Midsummer 1837 show that on April 10, William Caines, age 14, was committed for trial by Gustavus [sic] Smith Esq, 'charged with stealing at Honiton on the 8th inst, from the person of Agnes Richards, a purse containing money, to the amount of eleven shillings in silver'.

Stirling also mentions that Gustavius Smith Esq of Castle-hill, 'a handsome seat', was the principal proprietor in Sidbury, this of course being in the 1830s when Stirling wrote his book. It is interesting to ponder how such apparently wealthy gentry came to live in Fortfield Terrace: as they quite often subsequently moved elsewhere in Sidmouth it is possible that they rented until a suitable property came up for sale.

July 1851 saw the first of many advertisements relating to the Terrace, in *Harvey's Sidmouth Directory*:

```
              No 1 Fort Terrace, Sidmouth
 - TO BE LET furnished - for a few months, the above comfort-
   able and DESIRABLE RESIDENCE, with or without coach-house
                 and stable. Apply at the house.
```

In November of that year, medical opinion confirmed that the climate of Sidmouth was good for plants and people. W H Cullen MD wrote:

> *In corroboration of the general characteristic of the peculiarity of the climate of this locality, I may add the names of some of the tender exotics that live and flourish in the open air: The Myrtle attains a great size, some in the Fort Field being more than twenty feet high…*

> *The annual proportion of deaths to living is in Sidmouth 1 in 65.50 – Devon 1 in 58 – England 1 in 49.   The annual mortality per cent is in Sidmouth 1.52 – Devon 1.972 – England 2.187.   The proportion out of every 1000 who attain 70 years and upwards in England and Wales is 140, and in Sidmouth 199.*[2]

In January 1852 Sidmouth Parish Church received a new stone font, 'presented by Captain Fulford RN with the cordial co-operation of a few of his friends'.

In the early summer of 1853 Sir John and Lady Awdry stayed at No 8 for two months. Sir John was a former fellow of Oriel College, Oxford (Edward Copleston's college) and subsequently Chief Justice at the Supreme Court of Bombay. Rather unfairly, history will probably pay less attention to him than to a later family member, the Rev W V Awdry who wrote *Thomas the Tank Engine*.

Later that year *Harvey's* reported the renaissance of Sidmouth Cricket Club:

> **5 August 1853**   *The Sidmouth Cricket Club. We are gratified to find the Sidmouth Cricket Club revived, under the most favourable auspices; and that nearly the whole of the Gentlemen in Sidmouth and its neighbour-hood have become subscribing members. From the unequalled situation of the cricket field we have no doubt of its proving highly attractive to the lovers of this manly sport.*[3]

Unfortunately the renaissance of the Cricket Club coincided with the demise of *Harvey's Sidmouth Directory*, so information for the rest of the decade is rather sparse. However, the Cricket Club went from strength to strength, and is currently one of the top cricket clubs in Devon.

The following year, Edward Hughes Ball Hughes leased No 1 Fortfield Terrace to Mrs Anne Jewell, for fourteen years at £35 per annum. Mrs Jewell lived at Retreat Cottage in Church Street, and leased No 1 as a business venture, as this advertisement in *Trewman's Exeter Flying Post* of 2 September, 1858 shows.

SIDMOUTH

TO BE LET, with possession at Michaelmas next,
No. 1 FORTFIELD TERRACE
Furnished; consisting of double drawing room, dining room, six bed rooms, water closet, kitchen, butler's pantry, housekeeper's room, scullery, larder, wine cellar, hard and soft water, flower garden, coach-house, and two-stalled stable.

Apply to Mrs Jewell, Retreat Cottage.

In the same year as that advertisement appeared, the original sixty year lease on No 8, made when the building of the Terrace was still being completed, came to an end. Documents at Devon County Records Office show that Edward Hughes Ball Hughes then leased No 8 to Alfred Lester for 21 years. No 8 was described as a dwelling house, garden, coach house and stables and the rent was £63 per annum. The house deeds name Alfred's unmarried daughter Mira as the leaseholder: she was the 'Miss Lester' who showed Peter Orlando Hutchinson the Sidmouth Manor Estate auction advertisement in chapter four.

In 1859 the leasing of No 7 by Edward Hughes Ball Hughes to John Webber for 5 years at £42 10s per annum brought a decade's business dealing in the Terrace to an end.

Through most of this decade the Leslie family were living at No 10. Robert Leslie is, as far as I know, the only Fortfield Terrace resident so far to have published his or her autobiography.

🙰 ROBERT CHARLES LESLIE 🙐

ROBERT C LESLIE
from 'A Waterbiography'

Robert Leslie was born in London in 1826. His father, Charles Robert Leslie, was an exceptional artist, who was a friend of many famous artists and authors of the time, including John Constable, Charles Dickens and William Makepeace Thackeray. He wrote a biography of John Constable.

Robert also was a gifted painter, and some of his works were exhibited at the Royal Academy. However, he had a rather relaxed attitude to education and life, describing his childhood as 'one long holiday, mostly spent on the banks of suburban ponds and canals sailing home-made model boats'. His passion for boats and the sea was the main influence on the pattern of his life.

In 1834 he 'made the acquaintance of' J W M Turner and spent some time by the lake at Lord Egremont's house at Petworth watching him make a model sailing ship out of a bit of board and some scraps of paper and launching it on the lake. Sixteen years later he met the great man at the Royal Academy, and was pleased that Turner passed positive comment on one of his paintings.

In 1849 he married Eliza, a childhood friend recently widowed and with an income which enabled them to indulge his whims. So it was that Robert and Eliza moved to Sidmouth in 1851 with their two small sons, Henry and Robert, and lived at No 10, Fortfield Terrace.

Robert wrote his autobiography in 1894, entitled *A Waterbiography*, which contains an account of his years in Sidmouth, though this concentrates almost entirely on boats and the sea.[4]

In his account he talks about his early meeting with one of the Sidmouth fishermen, Harry Conant, who lent him his boat, 'England's Rose', and with whom he formed a great friendship. Then, as now, running a fishing boat from the beach at Sidmouth was not easy. Robert spent the next few years building boats on Sidmouth beach. His first, 'Foam', was a fifteen-footer, and he writes of her exploits through calm and storm with great affection.

He describes the first Sidmouth Regatta particularly well – an event dominated by appalling weather, in which the spectators on shore were unable to see the boats, and the sailors on the boats were unable to see the mark-boats, let alone the shore.

SIDMOUTH REGATTA by Robert C Leslie
from 'A Waterbiography'

Subsequently, he spent two years building a forty-five footer, with the help of a local boat-builder. The keel and planking came from an elm tree close to Fortfield Terrace, found by the boat-builder. In his own words:

> *There is that great ellum in Farmer Grip's orchard hedge, which, if it don't open full of ramping big knots, which 'edge ellums is liable to, will cut our keel in one, and what's left of the clean tough butt ought to make enough inch stuff to half plank her bottom.*

Then, as now, felling large trees was beset with administrative difficulties. The tenant farmer would be:

> *glad to be rid of the toady ellum what's been killing of two of his best red-streaked apple-trees for years; but it don't lay along of he; and Miss C his landlady can't abide to cut a stick of timber.*[5]

I think a conversation between Robert Leslie's boat-builder and Elizabeth Barrett Browning on the subject of Sidmouth's elms (see page 51) would have been amusing. Anyway, the tree was felled, and the boat built and named 'Rip Van Winkle'. The name, Leslie says, was chosen 'because in her we first really drifted clear of or away from a long, sleepy twelve years' repose in the Valley of the Sid. We might perhaps have effected an escape by other means, but they did not occur to us, or we wanted the energy to use them'. They were not the first or last to fall under the enchantment of Sidmouth.

Eliza was a very tolerant wife: she 'never cared for the sea', but indulged Robert in his passion for it. Their daughter, Katherine, was born in Sidmouth, presumably at Fortfield Terrace, in 1853. Eliza must have been happy in Sidmouth, for after returning to 'our happy west-country valley' from a cruise across the Atlantic, she said that she thought she would never feel uncomfortable again.

The family eventually drifted clear of Sidmouth in 1863 in 'Rip Van Winkle', finally settling in Southampton, where Robert died in 1901.

☙   GREAT EXPECTATIONS   ❧

1860 - 1869

This was a decade of progress, interspersed with a few less creditable episodes. In all honesty, most decades of human history are probably like that.

In **1860** Charles Dickens wrote *Great Expectations,* and as it was for his hero Pip, not everything in the wider world turned out quite as expected. On the plus side, **1861** saw the emancipation of serfs in Russia, for which our Grand Duchess Helena had campaigned for much of her life. The same year, across the Atlantic, eleven states broke away from the Union to form the Southern Confederacy and start the American Civil War, which lasted till 1865. In Britain that year, following hard on the heels of *On The Origin Of Species,* came another life-changing publication, Mrs Beeton's *Book Of Household Management*. Finally in 1861 Queen Victoria's beloved Prince Albert died, as did our very own poetess, Elizabeth Barrett Browning. In **1863** the first underground railway opened in London, and in Paris Edward Hughes Ball Hughes, Lord of Sidmouth Manor, died. In **1864,** five years after the death of Isambard Kingdom Brunel, his Clifton Suspension Bridge was opened in Bristol (a bridge later considered by my grandmother to be 'an unnecessary risk').

1865 was the year in which slavery was abolished in the United States and President Abraham Lincoln was assassinated. In Oxford, Lewis Carroll wrote *Alice's Adventures In Wonderland*. Back in Russia, in 1865 Leo Tolstoy wrote *War And Peace* and in **1886** Fyodor Dostoevski wrote *Crime And Punishment*. Following the production of these literary landmarks, in **1867** Russia sold Alaska to the USA for $7 million, in retrospect perhaps not the best business transaction of all time. Back in Britain, in **1868** Disraeli became Prime Minister, and that year saw also the first meeting of the National Society for Women's Suffrage and the first Trades Union Congress. In **1869** the Suez canal opened, linking East and West and opening up the possibilities for more trade and colonization.

The 1861 census lists the following residents of Fortfield Terrace on the night of Sunday, April 7:

1	John Ingleby-Mackenzie	Head	Married	27	General Practitioner MB BS (Cambridge)	Middlesex
	Emily E Ingleby-Mackenzie	Wife	Married	21		Bombay
	Helen Ingleby-Mackenzie	Daughter		7m		St Pancras
	Jane Court	Servant	Single	25	Nurse	Somerset
	Elizabeth Bartlett	Servant	Single	21	Housemaid	Exeter
	Isabella Bartlett	Servant	Single	16	Under Housemaid	Sidbury
1 ½	Caroline Copplestone	Head	Single	72	Annuitant	Devon
	Catherine Blake	Companion	Single	38		Ireland
	Louisa Parsons	Servant	Single	36	Servant	Devon
	Sarah Hutchings	Servant	Single	23	Servant	Devon
	Jemmima Collacott	Servant	Single	21	Servant	Devon
2	Hon Charlotte Mary Shore	Head	Widow	60	Fundholder	Sidmouth
	Emma Ruding	Friend	Single	44	Fundholder	St Pancras
	Ann Anning	Servant	Single	35	Servant	Bovey Tracey
	Ann Lock	Servant	Single	35	Servant	Bishops-teignton
	Mary Horn	Servant	Single	22	Servant	Sidmouth
5	Fanny Pemberton	Head	Single	39	House Proprietor	Ireland
	Elizabeth Pyne	Servant	Single	23	General Servant	Sidbury
6	Mary Newman	Head	Widow	65	Lodging House Keeper	Sidmouth
	Edward Newman	Son	Single	21	Baker	Sidmouth
	Ellen Dean	Servant	Single	20	Servant	Sidford
	Mary Jane Maye	Lodger	Single	64	Annuitant	Wiltshire
	Elizabeth Ann Gover	Servant	Single	34	Servant	Sidmouth
	Richard Taylor	Head	Married	37	Pensioner	Middlesex
	Sarah Taylor	Wife	Married	33		Whitwell
	Edwin Nott	Visitor	Single	47	House Proprietor	Thames Ditton
7	Anne Hopkins	Head	Widow	68	Fundholder	Westbury
	Anne Cockell	Niece	Single	33		Leigh, Wilts
	Mary Gertrude Cockell	Niece	Single	17		Staple Ashton
	Ann Pike	Servant	Single	23	House Servant	Sidmouth
	Sarah Masters	Servant	Single	27	House Cook	Longload
8	Mary Jane Kennett Dawson	Head	Widow	62	Fundholder	Middlesex
	Richard Kennett Dawson	Son	Single	39	Landed Proprietor	Frickley Hall
	Benjamin Kennett Dawson	Son	Single	25		Sidmouth
	Catherine Kennett Dawson	Daughter	Single	42		Frickley Hall
	Frances Kennett Dawson	Daughter	Single	40		Bath
	Mary B Harding	Servant	Single	27	Parlour Maid	Devon
	Sarah Ann Best	Servant	Single	24	Cook	Exeter
	Anne Godding	Servant	Single	16	House Maid	Exeter
9	William H Mercer	Head	Married	47	Lt Col Indian Army	Plymouth
	Maria U Mercer	Wife	Married	28		Cape of Good Hope
	Fanny Maria Mercer	Daughter		4	Scholar	Worcester
	Harry Mercer	Son	Single	2		Sidmouth
	Charlotte Carter	Servant	Single	19	Nurse	Sidmouth
	Grace Rogers	Servant		22	Housemaid	Dartmouth
10	Robert C Leslie	Head	Married	34	Artist Marine Painter	Middlesex
	Eliza Jane Leslie	Wife	Married	34	Fundholder	Middlesex
	Henry Leslie	Son		10	Scholar	Blackheath
	Robert Leslie	Son		9	Scholar	Middlesex
	Katherine Jane Leslie	Daughter		8	Scholar	Sidmouth
	Martha Hill	Servant	Single	21	Housemaid	Salcombe R
	Katherine Hill	Servant	Single	23	Cook	Salcombe R

Nos 3 and 4 were unoccupied. Amongst the usual crop of luminaries including Miss Coppleston, doctors, assorted Kennet-Dawsons, landed gentry and retired Army Colonels, we find for the first time lodging-house keepers, and No 6 being described as 'Mrs Newman's Lodgings'.

The Hon. Mrs Charlotte Mary Shore (née Cornish) at No 2 deserves special mention as a local, the niece of Hubert Cornish who painted the Long Picture of Sidmouth (see chapter four). She married the Hon. Frederick Shore, who worked in the Bengal Civil Service, and whose father, John Shore 1st Baron Teignmouth was Governor General of Bengal. Sadly Frederick died in 1837 after only seven years of marriage.

Great expectations were attached to the possibility of the Railway coming to Sidmouth. By 1862 The Sidmouth Railway and Harbour Act was going through parliament. The idea was to build a harbour at the Eastern end of the Promenade, with a railway line running up the East of the valley, to connect the harbour with the mainline at Feniton. Locally, the scheme was generally deemed to be A Good Thing but there were concerns about finance and the cost to shareholders. The Act was passed in August.

There were, however, more pressing issues troubling the residents of Sidmouth. In May 1862, a report appeared in *Lethaby's Sidmouth Journal* under the (remarkably familiar) heading: 'A Public Grievance – lack of Public Conveniences'. This bemoaned the fact that people were relieving themselves in inappropriate places in the town:

> No doubt, as was remarked at the meeting, much of the evil may be attributed to the lack of training by parents and others, so that children are allowed and encouraged to do that publicly, and with impunity, which better training would teach to avoid.[1]

More public grievance concerned the state of footpaths:

> To see the condition in which the paths near the Fort Field on one side, and those leading from Radway in every direction on the other, are frequently found, is surely sufficient to convince the most resolute and sturdy economist.[1]

On a more positive note the Committee for the Improvements of Sidmouth accounts showed income of £20 'by one Year's Rent for Pasturage for Sheep in Fortfield', and continuing the positive theme, *The Leisure Hour* of 11 October, 1862, under the title 'Less Frequented Watering Places', reported that:

> Sidmouth is decidedly the queen of all the seaside places on this coast, and nothing but its location so far out of the railway system has prevented this from being acknowledged. There is a noble cricket ground, and a public promenade called the Fortfield in front of the sea...There is excellent bathing, and a row of lodging-houses facing the sea, with a lawn in common before them... [2]

But in case we get carried away by the excellence of the bathing, this letter was published in *Lethaby's Journal* in June 1864.

> To the Editor of the Sidmouth Journal. Sir, - From what I had read in your Journal and the Directory, I was in hope that the scandal of last year, arising from the bathing question, had been removed. However, I see that a material part of the objection still remains, viz., the ladies' machines and the fishing boats being in close contiguity. If the arrangement is not altered, you may rest assured that very few visitors will frequent the place for the purpose of bathing; and while I remain here I will take care that my wife and daughters shall not be annoyed as they were last year. I am, Sir, your's [sic] faithfully, A FRIEND TO SIDMOUTH.[3]

A Friend To Sidmouth would have been annoyed to see this photograph, probably taken a few years later. It does emphasise the possible tensions between leisure and industry in seaside towns, which are still highlighted today in letters to *The Sidmouth Herald*. One person's holiday haven is another person's place of work.

SIDMOUTH PROMENADE

During this period, the readers of the Journal were also kept informed about events across the Atlantic, as the American Civil War entered its fourth year.

In August 1864 work finally began on the Feniton Branch Line, and leisure activities continued on the Fortfield, with the Cricket Club meeting on Monday and Thursday afternoons at 2.30, and the Amateur Cricket Club meeting on Wednesday evenings at 6 o'clock.

And then there was archery...

ARCHERY AT SIDMOUTH
by Colonel Hawker
Sidmouth Museum

Having obtained the lease for No 7 Fortfield Terrace in 1859, Mr Webber was marketing it as a long-term let:

```
                    ELIGIBLE OPPORTUNITY
               7 Fortfield Terrace, Sidmouth.
   TO BE LET, the above Well-Furnished good FAMILY RESIDENCE,
containing Entrance Hall, two Reception Rooms, and five or six
  Bedrooms; together with a good Garden, and all necessary and
                      convenient Offices.
  A permanent Tenant would be preferred, as the premises have
 been in the occupation of two tenants only during the last
                        fourteen years.
      Apply to Mr WEBBER, Fore Street. (Shopkeeper)
```

In February 1865 letters to *Lethaby's Journal* highlighted two particular hazards on the Fortfield: men and boys shooting birds, and winter top-dressing with particularly offensive manure. The *Journal* drew attention to another more general menace:

> *Attention has been called to the plague of dogs with which Sidmouth, as well as other places, is troubled. We are credibly informed that there are nearly 250 in the town...*[4]

In April, a plan was published to alter the site of the railway terminus to Bulverton and to abandon the harbour idea. (I wonder if a harbour scheme will ever be resurrected?)

Following the death of the Lord of Sidmouth Manor, Edward Hughes Ball Hughes, in 1863, in July 1866 the whole of the Sidmouth Manor Estate was put up for sale, with the following advertisement:[5]

SIDMOUTH
SOUTH COAST OF DEVON

Mr Ovenden has been favoured with instructions to offer FOR SALE by Private Contract, either in their entirety or in lots, the ESTATES of the late Edward Hughes Ball Hughes, Esq., situate at and near Sidmouth, in the county of Devon, and comprising the ancient MANOR of Sidmouth, with the manorial rights, and about 600 acres of agricultural and building land, for the most part highly productive; a large portion of the Town of Sidmouth, including nearly the whole sea frontage, and comprising the principal hotel, the town-hall, the market-house, and market tolls, together with the residence of His Royal Highness the late Duke of Kent, and a great number of dwelling-houses, shops, and cottages.

The town of Sidmouth overlooks one of the most beautiful bays on the south-west coast of England, and is surrounded on the land side by highly picturesque and richly wooded hills, from which views of almost unequalled beauty can be obtained. The air is extremely salubrious, and the town has been for nearly a century the resort, during both the summer and the winter seasons, of visitors of the highest class. The agricultural land is of very excellent quality, and the natural conformation of the ground renders it possible to appropriate large tracts for building purposes, and to secure to the houses which may be erected the advantage of extensive and varied sea and land views, while it also affords a choice of several positions, each admirably adapted for the site of a mansion and park. The construction of a railway, to connect Sidmouth with the South-Western Line, has been commenced.

Printed particulars are in course of preparation, and may shortly be obtained on application to Mr. OVENDEN, land agent and surveyor, 55, Lincoln's Inn Fields, W.C.

In October of that year Dr Taylor Warry, once resident at No 4, died on his way to All Saints Church, and in November the Rev Dr Heneage Gibbes, the Vicar of All Saints, and Mrs Gibbes moved into No 10.

The owner of the freehold of No 2 since 1817, Rev James Hobson, had died in 1860 and his wife Sarah in 1861. No 2 was acquired by the Rev Arthur Marmaduke Franklin Browne who, in 1866, sold it to Mr John Darby.

1866 ended with vandalism in Fortfield Terrace, as recorded in *Lethaby's Journal*:

> *DASTARDLY OUTRAGE – We regret to learn that a cowardly and wanton act of damage was committed early in December, in Fortfield Terrace (No 3). A large stone was thrown against Dr Miller's back parlour window, with force sufficient to have injured life or limb, but fortunately the family were sitting in another room. What motive there could be for the act, except that of a love of mischief, cannot be imagined, as the worthy Doctor has not a known enemy in the town; but, on the contrary, many hearty wishers for his better health.*[6]

On August 31, 1867, G E Balfour of Manchester completed his purchase of the Sidmouth Manor Estate, and so Fortfield Terrace again changed ownership. There was general optimism that the change of ownership would improve things.

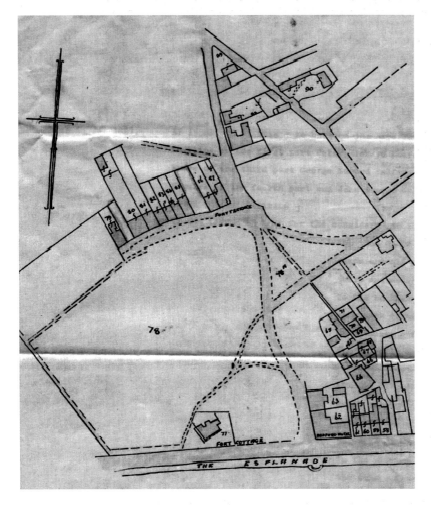

MANOR ESTATE PLAN OF FORTFIELD TERRACE 1867

This map from 1867 shows some of the Manor Estate including Fortfield Terrace, with the estate numbers. Nos 2 and 9 are unnumbered, having been in separate ownership since before 1820.

Throughout 1868 Mr Webber was working hard to market No 7, perhaps with an increasing note of anxiety:

> **January**
> SIDMOUTH To Be Let Furnished, with immediate possession, an excellent FAMILY HOUSE, No 7, Fortfield Terrace; Which has been thoroughly repaired and renovated. Apply to Mr Webber, Fore Street.

> **October**
> SIDMOUTH. TO BE LET, Furnished, for the 6 Winter Months, to a small Family, for 60 Guineas, the excellent Winter Residence, No 7, Fortfield Terrace. Apply to Mr Webber, Fore Street.

> **November**
> SIDMOUTH. TO BE LET, Furnished, for the 6 Winter Months, to a small Family, for 40 Guineas, the excellent Winter Residence, No 7, Fortfield Terrace. Apply to Mr Webber, Fore Street.

In October 1868 advertisements appeared in *Lethaby's Journal* for 'Stereoscopic Views of Sidmouth and its environs by F Bedford, W Bray, etc., price 1 shilling'. This is Francis Bedford's stereoview of Fortfield Terrace:

I think that these are among the earliest photographs of Fortfield Terrace. They capture a relaxed atmosphere: one where people had time to stop and talk. Rather like Sidmouth today…

FORTFIELD TERRACE 1868
photograph by Francis Bedford

Finally, as the decade came to an end, in July 1869, after an illness of several months, the new Lord of the Manor, G E Balfour, Esq., died in London. The editorial in *Lethaby's Journal* suggested that he was not liked locally, and did nothing for the Estate other than raising rents and ending tenancies. Government figures showed that at the time of his death, the Sidmouth Manor Estate consisted of 690 acres, with an annual gross rental income of £2,267. The Estate was to be held in trust until such time as his son, J E H Balfour achieved his twenty-fifth birthday.

❧ THE KENNET DAWSONS ❧

The Kennet Dawsons were prominent members of the Sidmouth community in the second half of the nineteenth century and had associations with the Terrace in various combinations between 1849 and 1875. They originated from Frickley Hall in Yorkshire, and from the census records it appears that at least part of the family moved down to Sidmouth in the 1830s.

In 1849, Frances Mary Kennet-Dawson (54), born in Wakefield, and her sister, Jane Kennet-Dawson (41), born in Sandal Magna, were living at No 7 Fortfield Terrace where they stayed until at least 1853. They were both unmarried, the original 'Misses Dawson'.

In 1861 their sister-in-law, the widowed Mary Ann Kennet-Dawson (62), born in Middlesex, was living at No 8, with four children, Catherine (42), born at Frickley Hall, Frances Ellen (40), born in Bath, Richard (39), born at Frickley Hall and Benjamin (25) born in Sidmouth. Catherine and Frances (Ellen) were unmarried and were the second 'Misses Dawson'. By 1862 Benjamin was no longer living with them, and the rest of the family moved in 1863.

Miss Jane Kennet-Dawson died in 1872 at Cotlands at the age of 68, and her sister Frances in 1874, age 80, also at Cotlands.

CATHERINE & FRANCES KENNET-DAWSON
by Col Hawker Sidmouth Museum

In 1871 Mary Ann and her family were living at Bedford House. She died in 1872 (seven months before her sister-in-law Jane) at the age of 73. In 1875 the second Misses Dawson spent two months at No 1 Fortfield Terrace.

In *A Story Of Sidmouth*, Anna Sutton recalls of Powys House (on the corner of All Saints Road and Station Road): 'My first memory of it is when my godmother, Miss Dawson, lived there with her sister. I was very small at the time'. And of Audley (on the opposite side of All Saints Road), which as we have seen was built by the Dowager Lady Jane, she says, 'Audley Cottage was enlarged and converted from a thatched cottage by the Misses Dawson, who made it into an elegant building'.[7]

On 27 July, 1892 *The Sidmouth Observer and Visitors' List* reported the death at Powys of Miss Frances Ellen Kennet-Dawson age 72. Wreaths and flowers included a message from her sister Catherine, 'Dearest Ellen from her loving sister', and one from Miss Blake of 1½ Fortfield Terrace 'with affectionate remembrance'.[8]

CHAPTER TWELVE
1870 - 1879

✥ DISCOVERY ✥

1870 - 1879

This was the decade in which the positive activities of the Manor and the arrival of the railway transformed Sidmouth and enabled its discovery by the wider world. It was also a time of invention and innovation.

For Britain it was a decade of relative peace and increasing prosperity. In **1870** France declared war on Prussia. France was heavily defeated and Paris was occupied. In that year Charles Dickens died. In **1871** France and Prussia signed a peace treaty, Lewis Carroll wrote *Through The Looking Glass, And What Alice Found There*, and Stanley discovered Livingstone on the shore of Lake Tanganyika. In **1872** there was a smallpox epidemic in London: in fact, between 1871 and 1873 in England and Wales 44,840 people died of smallpox at a time when it was estimated that 97 percent of the population had been vaccinated. In **1873** Britain defended her colonial interests in the Gold Coast. Parliament reduced the working week to 56.5 hours in **1874**, the same year that Tolstoy wrote *Anna Karenina* and Jesse Boot opened his first shop in Nottingham.

It was as late as **1875** that the use of boys as chimney sweeps was outlawed. In the same year Disraeli's government bought enough shares in the Suez Canal to give Britain a controlling interest. In **1876** Queen Victoria was declared Empress of India, Alexander Graham Bell invented the telephone, and Mark Twain wrote *Tom Sawyer*. In **1877** Britain annexed the Boer Republic of Transvaal, and across the Atlantic Thomas Edison invented the phonograph. In another move destined to create long-term problems, in **1878** Britain and Turkey signed a secret treaty allowing Britain to occupy Cyprus in return for help against the Russians. That year London turned on its electric street-lights for the first time. **1879** was the year of the Zulu Wars, bringing to the British public names like *Isandlwana* and *Rorke's Drift*. Total casualties on the British side were 1,727 and on the Zulu side over 10,500.

Readers of *The Sidmouth Directory and General Advertiser* in 1870 were saddened to hear of the death of Charles Dickens, who even then was a bit of a national institution, and were interested to read about the Franco-Prussian War, safely distant on the other side of the Channel.

Commercial life in Fortfield Terrace continued with this advertisement:

```
    TO BE LET Unfurnished from Midsummer, an excellent
family residence being No 2 Fortfield Terrace consisting
   of large Dining Room, Parlour, Double Drawing Room,
  Breakfast Room, 7 Bedrooms, 2 Dressing Rooms, with all
necessary offices. Apply to Mr Henry Dawe, Grocer; or to
               Mr W G Harris, the Balsters
```

Later that year tenders were invited 'for the formation of a pebble gutter by the side of the dwarf wall of the Fortfield, from Fort Cottage to Fortfield Terrace', up what is now Station Road, adjacent to the croquet pitches. Three estimates were forthcoming, as follows:

> *Mr P Evans, 16 inches wide, 3½ d. per yard, the Board supplying materials; or 7d. including materials. Mr S Goss, 15 inches wide, 3d. per yard. Messrs. Piper and Son, the same width and price.*[1]

As ever, not everyone quoted to the same specification, but the contract was awarded to Mr Goss.

Lethaby's Journal of 1 December, 1870 confirmed that the new railway would terminate midway between Bulverton and Broadway. A new road was proposed to go from the station, behind Broadway, down Bickwell Valley, and then 'skirting the end house of Fortfield Terrace, and going in a diagonal line across the Fortfield, to the corner opposite the Bedford Hotel.' The article concluded with the question, 'What will the town say to such a proposal as that?' to which I suspect that then, as now, the answer would have conveyed something less than enthusiasm.[2]

Presumably, polite responses from cricketers, residents of Fortfield Terrace and other interested parties having been received, in February 1871 it was proposed at the Local Board that 'the railway approach road should be brought out in front of Fortfield Terrace, instead of being carved through the Fort Field', ending 'in the present road in front of Fortfield Terrace.'[3] No doubt this brought forth another flurry of objections. Rather belatedly, general unhappiness was expressed about the siting of the station 'nearly a mile from the beach' and 'virtually unapproachable by three-fourths of the inhabitants of the town and neighbourhood'.

The 1871 census of April 2 listed the following:

1	Margaret Dunn	Head	W	49	Pensioner	Scotland
	Frances Dunn	Daughter		14	Scholar	Devon Stonehouse
	Margaret Dunn	Daughter		10	Scholar	Devon Stonehouse
	Richard Dunn	Brother-in-law	M	54	JP	St Albans
	Eliza Dunn	Sister-in-law	M	54		Weymouth
	Rebecca Risk	Governess	S	37	Governess	Newton Poppleford
	Laura Best	Servant	S	25	House Maid	Stockton
	Mary Hooper	Servant	S	44	Cook	
1 ½	Caroline Copplestone	Head	S	82	Annuitant	Offwell
	Catherine Blake	Friend	S	51	Annuitant	Galway Ireland
	Eliza Manley	Servant	S	31	House Maid	Sidmouth
	Emma Hunt	Servant	S	41	Needlewoman	
4	Harriet Cartwright	Head	W	49	Lodging House Keeper	Salcombe Regis
	Emily Cartwright	Daughter	S	18	Assistant	Bristol
	Ellen Gorham	Lodger	S	35		Bedfordshire
	Maria Kerr	Lodger	W	70	Annuitant	Galway Ireland
6	Miss Lester (absent)	Head				
	Charlotte Pritchard	Visitor	S	19	[Hand Holder]	Shrewsbury
	Mary Leach	Servant	M	53	Cook	Dorset
	Mandy Leach	Servant	S	43	Domestic	Sidmouth
	Sarah Lockyer	Servant	S	24	Domestic	Ottery St Mary
8	John Giles	Head	M	58	Barrister	Lambeth
	Charlotte Giles	Wife	M	54		Lancashire
	Agnes Giles	Daughter	S	25		Lambeth
	Isabella Giles	Daughter	S	23		Lambeth
	Charlotte Giles	Daughter		12	Scholar	Gloucester
	Ann Halton	Servant	M	43	Domestic Servant	Sidmouth
	Elizabeth Bond	Servant	S	23	Domestic Servant	Sidmouth
	Ellen Salter	Servant	S	23	Domestic Servant	Bradninch
	Mary Grist	Servant	S	27	Domestic Servant	Sidbury
9	Edmund Butcher	Head	W	79	Lodging House Keeper	Islington
	Harriet Russell	Servant		45	Cook and Housekeeper	
	Ellen Russell	Servant		14	Domestic Servant	
	James Selly	Nephew to housekeeper		11	Visitor and scholar	Cambridge

Nos 2, 3, 5, 7 and 10 were unoccupied on census night. Miss Caroline Copleston was, of course, still in residence. Miss Lester, though obviously very involved in Terrace affairs over many years, managed to avoid all the censuses. It is sadly inevitable that we know so little about many of the people who made up the community of Fortfield Terrace that April night. We do know that Major Dunn had died at No 1 in December 1870 at the age of 43. And we know quite a lot about Edmund Butcher at No 9, to whom we shall return.

During this period the Trustees of the Manor Estate were trying to reverse the decline of decades of neglect. As you may recall, in 1816 the freehold of No 2 was sold by the Manor to the Rev James Hobson. Having passed through the ownership of the Rev Arthur Marmaduke Franklin Browne, Mr John Darby and George Henry Garrard, No 2 was finally sold to John Heugh, a trustee of the Manor, bringing it back into the Manor Estate.

Lethaby's reported the death of Gustavus Smith JP on 30 April, 1871 at Salcombe Mount (now the Hunter's Moon Hotel).[4] His wife, Jane, died a year later.

There was a good clear out at No 7, advertised in *The Sidmouth Directory and General Advertiser* on September 18:

> **No 7 Fort Field Sidmouth**
> The sale at auction by Messrs Farrant and Hussey will take place on Monday and Tuesday next, 25th and 26th inst. For all the Neat and Valuable Furniture of three Reception, and 5 bed and other rooms, also Kitchen and culinary articles of every description, as per Sale bill. No reserve. Lease of house expired.

In 1873 the Rev Edmund Lyde Butcher sold the freehold of No 9 to John Heugh, acting on behalf of the Manor, and so for the first time since 1816 the whole of Fortfield Terrace had the same owner. So it stayed until the next century.

It was around this time that the Terrace had a change of appearance. It seems that until this point the façades of some of the houses were in the original red brick and some had white-washed or white stucco façades. There were balconies only on Nos 7 and 8. This is the 'before' picture:

FORTFIELD TERRACE c. 1870 Sidmouth Museum

The Sidmouth Directory of 1 November, 1873 records:

> *Writing of improvements, we must not omit those effected in the appearance of the two last houses on Fortfield Terrace. With their verandahs and stuccoed fronts they quite eclipse their neighbours, and incite a wish that the whole of the Terrace may be similarly and uniformly treated, together with other houses in the neighbourhood.* [5]

Apart from the addition of balconies and a uniformly stuccoed façade, the raised pavement at the front was modified, so that the slope was removed and replaced with a retaining wall. This 'after' picture could not have been taken many years after the Francis Bedford photograph in the previous chapter, and shows the Terrace resplendent with white stucco and balconies.

FORTFIELD TERRACE POST-1873 Sidmouth Museum

The railway finally arrived in Sidmouth on 9 July, 1874, terminating as planned between Bulverton and Broadway. Eventually it was decided that the road from the station to the town should run straight down what is now Station Road, though concerns were expressed about the gradient for horse-drawn carriages. This was a significant moment in the development of Sidmouth, and opened up the whole town and Fortfield Terrace to a much broader clientele. *The London Standard* of 22 August summed this up very well:

The oldest watering-place on the Devonshire coast – yet in one sense, the very newest – is Sidmouth. It was 'discovered' by an occasional aristocratic visitor, long before the end of the last century. It has only within the last month or two been brought into contact with the world by means of a railway. At present Sidmouth is one of the pleasantest retreats on the southern coast.[6]

Possibly as a result of this, the following years featured numerous advertisements for rental opportunities in the Terrace, with Nos 4, 6 and 8 all seeking occupants and Nos 1, 2, 3 and 10 advertised as lodging-houses.

Facilities in Sidmouth developed. Appointments were available with Mr Maggs the visiting dentist from Yeovil, who could be contacted at No 4 Fortfield Terrace. Sidmouth (Roller) Skating Rink was open to the public on Mondays, Wednesdays and Saturdays from three to five o'clock. Admission was 1 shilling per person, or 12 tickets could be purchased for 8 shillings (including, fortunately, the use of skates).

A greater diversity of interesting advertisements started appearing in the journals.

```
    A Christian Young Person is desirous of getting a
  Situation as upper HOUSEMAID or to wait on an invalid
  Lady. Is a good plain needle-woman. Country preferred.
    Address, C Taylor, Chapel Street, Sidbury, Sidmouth,
                        Devon
```

```
    TO MEDICAL MEN, AND OTHERS. WANTED, a HOME for a
  LUNATIC. - A Gentleman, about 60 years of age, who has
  been in his present situation for some years, now wishes
  for a change. He must be visited by a Doctor, and he is
      under the control of the Lunacy Commissioners. The
      neighbourhood of Sidmouth would be preferred.
```

Residents of Fortfield Terrace continued to make their voice heard and to be ignored. At the Local Board meeting in July 1878:

A letter from Miss Lester [resident variously at Nos 6, 7 and 8] *was read, in reference to the closing of one of the gates of the Fortfield to the inconvenience of the inhabitants of the Terrace; but it did not appear to the Board to be a grievance of which they could take notice.[7]*

The decade ended with the building of the new cricket pavilion in 1879, built by Mr James Harris of Cotmaton, the design showing the structure to be:

A pretty, rustic building composed of fir poles with the rough bark on, and covered with thatch.[8]

SIDMOUTH CRICKET PAVILION c. 1879   Sidmouth Museum

❧ THE BUTCHERS ❧

The Butcher family had a long and interesting association with Sidmouth and Fortfield Terrace. Their story adds weight to the notion that once Sidmouth gets you under its spell, wherever you go and whatever you do, it eventually draws you back.

This account relates to three generations of the Butcher family including three Edmunds: The Rev Edmund Butcher, Edmund Butcher MD and the Rev Edmund Lyde Butcher.

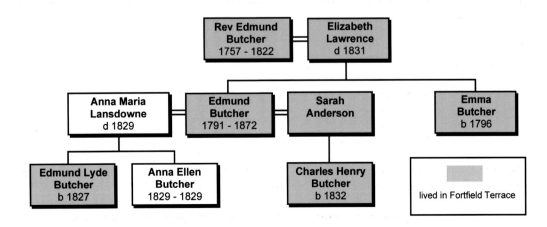

The Rev Edmund Butcher was born in 1757. He became a Unitarian Minister in London. He married Elizabeth (née Lawrence, a Shropshire family). Elizabeth had previously been married to Samuel Lowe and had four daughters, a son and a step-son before she married Edmund in the 1780s. Edmund and Elizabeth had two children, Edmund (born 1791) and Emma (born 1796). They seem to have been a close family. Rev Butcher wrote letters 'from a father to his daughter, the day after her coming of age - to Emma October 18, 1817' and 'Lines to Edmund Butcher on his thirtieth birthday by his father' on 4 July, 1821.

In 1797, due to the Rev Butcher's poor health, the family moved to Burcombe (possibly Burscombe) in Sidbury. He made a good recovery and in 1798 he became the Minister of the Sidmouth Unitarian Chapel.

> *The congregation did not become numerous under his care; he was not what is called a popular preacher; but it maintained a highly respectable character. Among his auditors were several who came to Sidmouth as visitors, and who were thankful to find a place where they could worship in spirit and in truth, and listen to discourses which, for piety, simplicity and general utility, were rarely equalled.*[9]

REV EDMUND BUTCHER
Old Dissenter Meeting House
Sidmouth

Apart from fulfilling his ministerial duties, Rev Butcher wrote several books, including the first *Guide Book to Sidmouth*, which we have already come across in Chapter Four. Other titles included:

> **1798** *Sermons: to which are subjoined, suitable hymns*
> **1801** *Moral Tales: designed to amuse the fancy and improve the hearts of the rising generation ... To which is added, by a Lady, The Unhappy Family; or, the dreadful effects of vice. A Tale.*
> **1803** *An excursion from Sidmouth to Chester, in the summer of 1803: In a series of letters to a lady. Includes sketches of the principal towns and villages ... Derby, Stafford, Warwick, and Worcester.*

1804 *Sidmouth scenery, or, Views of the principal cottages & residences of the nobility and gentry: With a description of that admired watering place and the environs, within fifteen miles round.*
1825 *Chronology of the kings of England in easy rhyme for Young People.* [Published posthumously]

Following his move to Sidmouth, some of his books were published by John Wallis, who owned Wallis' Library, to whom, over the years, he obviously felt some loyalty.

In Sidmouth rival libraries were set up by Mr. John Wallis (freshly down from London, the son of another John Wallis, a publisher there) and Mr. John Marsh. Both published Sidmouth guide books in which their own library was highly praised. That published by Mr. Marsh openly criticised Mr. Wallis's library: 'This building is on a more contracted scale; the views from it are good, but rather inferior to those of the library of Mr. John Marsh.' The Revd. Edmund Butcher, writing on behalf of Mr. Wallis, retaliated with other criticisms, clearly aimed at Mr. Marsh.[10]

Rev Butcher's ministry was particularly appreciated by Emmanuel Baruch Lousada, the owner of Peak House.

One gentleman there was, originally, of the Jewish persuasion, who became a permanent resident of Sidmouth, and who was so much pleased with Mr Butcher's society as well as ministerial services, that he presented him with a valuable piece of ground, near his own mansion, on which Mr Butcher built a house.[11]

It was on this land that Rev Butcher built Helen's (now St Helen's, Cotmaton Road), between 1807 and 1812. In 1817 he acquired the lease of No 3 Fort Terrace and, as we saw in Chapter 4, in 1819 that of No 9 Fort Terrace. Later in the same year he bought the freehold of No 9 from the Manor Estate.

Documents at Devon Records Office suggest that for at least part of 1820 he was living at No 9 Fort Terrace with his wife Elizabeth, and his son Edmund (then 27) and daughter Emma (22), although most of the time they probably resided at Helen's.

Rev Butcher's rent book, now at Bristol Records Office, shows the rent received from No 9 Fort Terrace around this time.

RENT BOOK
No 9 FORT TERRACE
1819 - 1821
Bristol Record Office

Rev Butcher's health failed again and in 1820 he left Sidmouth to live in Bath, where he died in 1822. The following memorial inscription is in the Unitarian Chapel in Sidmouth:

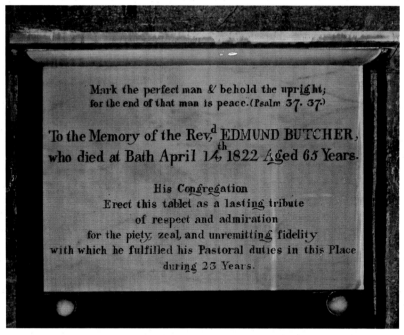

Mark the perfect man & behold the upright;
for the end of that man is peace.(Psalm 37. 37.)

To the Memory of the Rev.d EDMUND BUTCHER,
who died at Bath April 14th 1822 Aged 65 Years.

His Congregation
Erect this tablet as a lasting tribute
of respect and admiration
for the piety, zeal, and unremitting fidelity
with which he fulfilled his Pastoral duties in this Place
during 23 Years.

MEMORIAL INSCRIPTION FOR REV EDMUND BUTCHER
Old Dissenter Meeting House, Sidmouth

The Butcher story continues with Edmund Jr, who was 29 at the time of his father's death. It is likely that Edmund moved to Bristol when his parents moved to Bath. He was a doctor and also became an Alderman of the City of Bristol. Just three months before the death of his father he married Anna Maria Lansdowne. She was the daughter of John Lyde Lansdowne and Anna Maria Elderton, who lived in Jamaica and were in the sugar business.

Edmund kept a careful eye on the properties in Sidmouth and on his mother, who continued to move between Bath and Sidmouth, where she usually stayed at Helen's. So there are several letters from Edmund to his mother, in 1823 expressing satisfaction that No 9 was let, and in 1826 discussing the problems they were having with the tenants at Helen's, and a record of expenses for whitewashing done at No 9 Fort Terrace: six days work at 3 shillings per day.

In 1827 Edmund and Anna Maria had a son, Edmund Lyde and in 1829 they had a daughter, Anna Ellen Lawrence (the Lawrence presumably from Edmund's mother's family). All seemed to be going well, but sadly, on 22 April, 1829 Anna Maria died. In a letter with black border, Edmund wrote to his mother:

> *...if I can continue faithfully to do my duty to my dear Boy and Girl as I am now performing it, if not happiness, I may reckon upon gaining tranquilli-ty...* [12]

Shortly after this, his baby daughter, Anna Ellen died. Mother and daughter were buried in Christ Church, Bristol.

Both Edmund and his mother took great comfort from their faith during these times of loss. They continued to correspond regularly.

LETTER FROM EDMUND BUTCHER TO HIS MOTHER
Bristol Record Office

In 1831 Edmund's mother Elizabeth died, and also that year Edmund was married again, to Sarah Anderson. 1831 was a momentous year for him, as it was for Fortfield Terrace.

In 1831, the Reform Bill, designed to increase democracy in the country, was rejected by the Lords. Apart from making Mrs Partington famous, as we saw in Chapter 7, the rejection sparked unrest across the land. In Bristol riots took place, and in the ensuing suppression of the violence, several hundred people were killed. At the time Edmund Butcher was Chief Constable of St Michael's Ward in Bristol. The following year he was summoned to appear as a witness for the defence at the trial of the Mayor of Bristol, Charles Pinney, relating to his handling of the situation. The transcript of the trial suggests that Edmund did not actually testify.

In 1832 Edmund and Sarah had a son, Charles Henry Butcher. Edmund remained an Alderman of the City of Bristol until at least 1841.

At the beginning of 1851 Edmund and Sarah, with Edmund and Charles, moved back to No 9 Fortfield Terrace, Sidmouth. The 1851 census records Edmund's occupation as retired from the sugar trade. Their arrival was heralded by two advertisements in *Harvey's Journal* of 1 April, 1851:

```
No 9 Fortfield Terrace
                 Sidmouth
             CLASSICAL TUITION
Mr C H Butcher is desirous of obtaining as Pupils a few
Young Gentlemen under the age of sixteen, for instruc-
   tion in Greek, Latin, Mathematics, English, Etc.
                March 31, 1851
```

```
                   SIDMOUTH
Lessons in Drawing and Painting in Black lead,
            Water-colour or oil,
                     By
               Mr E L Butcher,
   Associate of the Bristol Fine Arts Academy.
       Testimonials of ability if required.
   9, Fort Field Terrace     March 31, 1851
```

The listing of Sidmouth professionals in June 1851 included Mr C H Butcher, Classical Tutor and Mr E L Butcher, Professor of Drawing and Painting. They stopped advertising in October 1852 and Edmund, Sarah and both sons left Sidmouth in November 1853. By 1861, Edmund Lyde Butcher was a curate in Gainford, Durham, married and with three children and went on to become Rector of Wolviston in Durham. Charles Henry Butcher was also a curate in 1861, and by 1884 was Dean of Shanghai.

Edmund reappeared at No 9 Fortfield Terrace in 1862 at the age of 70, but now on his own, so presumably Sarah had died in the intervening time. And there he spent the rest of his life, in relative obscurity for one who spent so much time in the public eye. As we have seen, in the 1871 census, Edmund, now 79, once doctor and city Alderman, was recorded as a lodging-house keeper, running No 9 with Harriet Russell (49), cook and housekeeper, and her daughter Ellen (14), domestic servant.

Lethaby's Journal of 1 August, 1872:

> *Died July 11 at 9 Fortfield Terrace, Edmund Butcher, Esq., formerly of London and Bristol, but long resident in Sidmouth; son of the Rev E Butcher, Author of the 'Beauties of Sidmouth, etc.', the first Guide-book of the town; aged 81 years.*[13]

And this is how it came to be that in 1873 Edmund Lyde Butcher sold No 9 Fortfield Terrace to the Manor Estate, not only bringing to an end the 54 year separation of No 9 from the Manor Estate, but also the involvement of the Butcher family in Fortfield Terrace.

CHAPTER THIRTEEN
1880 - 1889

❧ CELEBRATING OLD AND NEW ❧

1880 - 1889

The Education Act of **1880** made schooling in Britain compulsory up to the age of 10. Following the Zulu Wars in 1879, in December 1880 the first Anglo-Boer War started in South Africa, over the ownership of Transvaal. This skirmish lasted 4 months, ending with the Pretoria Convention and a compromise solution in **1881**. The 1881 census confirmed the growth of the professional and middle classes in Britain. Another colonial uprising in **1882** saw the Ashes of English Cricket taken to Australia. The Married Women's Property Act entitled married women, for the first time, to own property in their own right. In **1883** the Indonesian island of Krakatoa erupted, killing over 36,000 people, mostly as a result of tsunamis, and lowering average global temperatures for five years. There were spectacular sunsets around the world for months after the disaster. Robert Louis Stevenson published *Treasure Island* that year. In **1884,** entitlement to vote was extended to every householder with property worth more than £10, and Mark Twain wrote *Huckleberry Finn*.

In **1885** the internal combustion engine was invented, General Gordon died at Khartoum, and Britain and Russia were on the brink of war following the Russian seizure of Penjdeh in Afghanistan. **1886** saw Daimler produce the first motor-car. In a turbulent year in home politics the Salisbury government fell, Gladstone took over, was defeated on home rule for Ireland, and Salisbury was reinstated. As a bit of light relief, Britain annexed Upper Burma. In **1887** the Golden Jubilee of Queen Victoria was celebrated throughout the Empire and Conan Doyle wrote the first Sherlock Holmes story, *A Study In Scarlet*. **1888** was the year of Jack the Ripper and the founding of the English Football League, and George Eastman developed the Kodak camera. The decade came to an end with the building of the Eiffel Tower in Paris in **1889** for the Paris Centennial Exposition. Robert Browning, best known as the husband of Elizabeth Barrett Browning (who wrote about the hydrangeas in the garden of No 8 Fortfield Terrace), died. And in these imperial days the first shoots of a new world order appeared with the development of Coca-Cola in Atlanta, Georgia.

The decade got off to a shaky start with a report in *Lethaby's Journal* of vandalism in the Fort Field, with destruction of plants around the cricket pavilion, accompanied by the following stern sentiment, no doubt echoed by plant lovers and cricketers alike:

> *If the dastardly doer be convicted, as we trust he may be, small indeed will be the sympathy he will meet with, but hearty will be the hope that he may receive full punishment for his deeds.*[1]

Sadly, on 25 April, 1880, Mr John Webber, shop-keeper and confectioner, whom you may remember aggressively marketing No 7 Fortfield Terrace for rent in the 1860s, died at the age of 42, and fittingly an advertisement appeared just three weeks later in *Lethaby's:* 'TO LET furnished 7 Fortfield Terrace.'

In contrast to these unhappy stories, the magazine *Vanity Fair* carried an article about Sidmouth on 11 September from which this extract is taken:

> *Sidmouth is such a dear little place, with its lovely high rich-coloured cliffs, more like a country town than a watering-place; with one row of nice white houses in front of the sea, and heaps of pretty villas, in pretty gardens, farther away. So nice to live in, it looks to me like the place I have always been looking for, and sometimes dream about. Then there is a lovely Cricket ground, with one side to the sea, and lots of Lawn Tennis always going on there; and the people all know each other, and are so friendly and jolly.*[2]

As a tennis-playing resident of Sidmouth in 2012, I couldn't have put it better myself.

In 1881 Sidmouth Coffee House opened, which no doubt gave even more opportunity for friendliness and jollity.

SIDMOUTH PEOPLE
by Col Hawker
Sidmouth Museum

The 1881 census showed the following inhabitants of Fortfield Terrace at midnight on Sunday, April 3:

No.	Name	Relation		Age	Occupation	Birthplace
1	Phyllis Churchill	Head	W	58	Lodging House Keeper	Dean Prior
	Susan Furneaux	Niece	S	17		Buckfastleigh
	Clayton R E Leslie	Lodger	S	29	Lieut RN (Retired List)	London
	Kate Leslie	Sister	S	28	Annuitant	Sidmouth
1 ½	Catherine Blake	Head	S	62	Annuitant	Galway, Ireland
	Maria Kerr	Mother	W	80	Annuitant	Galway, Ireland
	Sarah A Hoskins	Servant	S	39	House and Parlour Maid	Sidmouth
	Jessie Holmes	Servant	S	34	Cook	Sidmouth
2	Thomas Fitzgerald	Head	M	46	Pensioner Chelsea	Limerick
	Mary Fitzgerald	Wife	M	42	Lodging House Keeper	Sidmouth
	Thomas Fitzgerald	Son		3	Scholar	Sidmouth
	Mary A Fitzgerald	Daughter		12	Scholar	Sidmouth
	Mary A Wyatt	Servant	S	29	Housemaid	Branscombe
	Cora Wyatt	Servant	S	27	Housemaid	Branscombe
	William M Floyd	Lodger	S	55	Annuitant	Brighton
	Fred Ingham	Lodger	M	23	Annuitant	Birmingham
	Alice Ingham	Wife	M	20	Annuitant	Birmingham
	Alice Davis	Servant	S	21	Lady's Maid	Gingemangan, Beds.
3	Harriet Cartwright	Head	W	59	Lodging House Keeper	Salcombe Regis
	Emily Cartwright	Daughter	S	28	Assistant Lodging House Keeper	St Pauls Bristol
4	Elizabeth Soloman	Head	M	50	Lodging House Keeper	Sidmouth
	Emily Gigg	Servant	S	19	General Servant	Sidmouth
	Grace Moore Hodder	Lodger	W	74	Domestic	Glasgow
	Harriet Hodder	Daughter	S	36	Annuitant	Rochester, Kent
	Felicity Hodder	Daughter	S	25	Annuitant	Cowes, IoW
					Annuitant	
5	William Martin	Head	W	80	Annuitant	Ireland
	Lucretia J Martin	Daughter	S	49	Annuitant	Ireland
	Mary J Page	Servant	S	24	Cook Domestic Servant	Sidmouth
	Emma Way	Servant	S	19	Housemaid Domestic Servant	Venn Ottery
6	Daniel Hook	Head	M	25	Fisherman	Sidmouth
	Emily Hook	Wife	M	29	Cook Domestic Servant	Trusham
7	Eliza S Woodfall	Head	W	64	Dividends	London
	Mary Hay	Daughter	M	32	Annuitant	Clifton, Gloucs
	Arabella Symons	Sister	S	53	Annuitant	Cornwall
	An Tufant	G'dson		3m		Stoke, Devon
	Ann Singer	Servant	S	53	Housekeeper	Scotland
	Miranda Burt	Servant	S	39	Lady's Maid	Cornwall, Madron
	Emily Allen	Servant	W	23	Nurse	Cornwall, Helston
	Elizabeth Staddon	Servant	S	36	General Servant	Cornwall, St Paul
	Susan Woodley	Servant	S	20	Kitchen Maid	Sidbury
	Sophy Parsons	Servant	S	16	Housemaid	Farway
	Jennie S Kember	Boarder		15	Scholar	Bath
	Nellie Palayzand	Boarder		12	Scholar	London
9	Thomas Slade	Head	M	35	Lodging House Keeper	Sidmouth
	Elizabeth Slade	Wife	M	38		Devizes
	Lucy Grayer	Servant	S	17	General Servant Domestic	Tiverton
10	Nathaniel K Parker	Head	M	53	Commercial Traveller for Brewer	Walton, Suffolk
	Sarah J K Parker	Wife	M	50	Lodging House Keeper	Freston, Suffolk
	Elizabeth C Parker	Daughter	S	21		Ipswich, Suffolk
	Alice Parker	Daughter	S	18		Ipswich, Suffolk
	Nathaniel H Parker	Son		14	Brewers' Apprentice	Freston, Suffolk
	Francis H Westlake	Lodger	W	64	Annuitant	Plymouth

No 8 was empty on census night. It was noted in the local papers that the number of uninhabited houses in Western Town (including Fortfield Terrace) had risen from 17 in 1871 to 23 in 1881. Nos 1, 2, 3, 4, 9 and 10 were, by this stage, designated as lodging-houses.

Clayton R E Leslie and his sister Kate were lodging at Mrs Churchill's, No 1 Fortfield Terrace for one week. They were two of the children of Robert Leslie, marine artist and sailor whom we met in Chapter Ten. I wonder if this was the first time they had returned to Sidmouth since leaving in 1863. Perhaps they were curious about the place where Kate had been born, and where they spent their early childhood.

Although they had been at No 2 since 1874, the Fitzgeralds appeared for the first time in a census, Mrs Fitzgerald being the lodging-house keeper for No 2. Mr Fitzgerald came from County Clare. He served in the Crimean War with the Royal Irish Regiment. Apparently he struck an officer and was court-martialled, remaining a private for 20 years. He married his Colonel's wife's maid who was from Sidmouth. Their son Thomas, 3 years old at the time of the census, went on to become Chairman of the Council, the owner of the Belmont Hotel, a notable cricketer and county rugby player, and president of the Devon Rugby Union. He was also the father of Brian Fitzgerald, who provided me with much of this information and died only a few years ago in his 90s.

The enigmatic Miss Lester managed to be absent from No 6 again on census night, but her cook, Emily, was present with her husband, Daniel Hook who was, of course, a fisherman by trade.

Residents of the Terrace from time to time during this decade included:

Mr Heugh, Trustee of the Manor Estate, and his wife at No 8: Mr and Mrs Da Ponte Player and their daughter at No 6 (possibly the artist F Da Ponte Player): General and Mrs Barrow at No 8: Lady Catherine Buchanan at No 2: Sir George E Wilson Couper, Bart., KCSI (ex-Lieutenant Governor of United Provinces, India), Lady Couper and family at No 2: General and Mrs Arbuckle and family at No 4: Sir Charles and Lady Margaret Domville at No 7:The Ayscoghe Floyers (part of the Cornish family) at No 7: the Very Rev Dean Butcher (of Cairo) at No 7. There are many others, who, though doubtless important to family members and friends, have not yet made it onto the Internet.

There were several Terrace related deaths:

> **18 January, 1884** *Death – On Friday 28th Dec, at Hartfield Grove, Sussex, the residence of her Son-in-law, Robert Melville Esq, ELIZA-BETH SHERWOOD WOODFALL, of [7] Fortfield Terrace, Sidmouth, widow of Lt Col George Woodfall, and daughter of William Symons Esq, of Hatt, Cornwall.*[3]

> **1 May, 1884** *Death in London of Major-General Charles Vaughan-Arbuckle (Late Royal Artillery) age 52. Served in Burma and the Crimea. (Relative of local resident, Mrs Hine-Haycock).* He and his family stayed at No 4 for three months at the beginning of the year.[4]

> **18 July, 1884** *Death - At 2 Fortfield Terrace, July 11 (suddenly) Thomas Fitzgerald aged 47 years* [Brian Fitzgerald's grandfather].[5]

> **1 August, 1884** *Died July 20 at Fortfield Terrace at the advanced age of 85 years, another of Sidmouth's oldest residents, Miss Joanna Bolton; a lady very much esteemed for her kindness, and her life-long purity of character.* Various members of the Bolton family had been resident in Fortfield Terrace over the previous twenty years.[6]

18 December, 1884   *Died December 16 at 10 Fortfield Terrace, Mr F H Westlake, aged 69 years.* He had lived at No 10 for 4 years.[7]

1 October, 1886   *Death in Isleworth of Dr George Miller age 76 'Though somewhat brusque in manner, he had a kindly heart'.* While living at No 3 Fortfield Terrace, he had a stone thrown through his back parlour window, though there is no evidence that this had anything to do with his bedside manner.[8]

1 December 1886   *Death on November 20 at 1½ Fortfield Terrace of Mrs Maria Kerr, widow of David Kerr Esq, Gentleman, age 86 years.* Maria Kerr was the mother of Miss Blake who was Caroline Copleston's companion at No 1½. [9]

Just in case one should think that people only come to Fortfield Terrace to die, there was one happier event, the birth of a daughter to Mr and Mrs J B Thomson who were spending four months at No 4. Ironically, but perhaps understandably, this rare event was recorded in the deaths section of *The Sidmouth Directory*.

In August 1881, during the Regatta and Sports Week, the circus was in town: it must have been quite a sight:

> *Sanger's unusually large and attractive Circus, with nearly a hundred horses, camels, elephants, etc, was encamped in the Higher Fortfield, at the rear of the Cricket Pavilion.*[10]

This painting by Henry Hasseler gives a good idea of the space behind the Fort Field, known as Back Fortfield, which had still not been developed at this stage.

BACK FORTFIELD FROM CUNNINGHAM'S LANE
by Henry Hasseler 1816 Sidmouth Museum

In January 1882 reference was made to the asphalt tennis court on the western side of the cricket pavilion, and later that year plans continued to develop the area where the circus had been:

> **18/05/1882** *LOCAL BOARD – Mr Orchard, on behalf of the Manor Trustees, produced a plan of certain deviations of the footpaths in Back Fortfield, and read the request of the Manor Trustees in reference thereto. It was considered that the trustees had greatly improved that locality, and that the proposed alterations would be a further improvement, and it was therefore unanimously resolved that the proposals made by Mr Orchard be acceded to, it being agreed that the footpath leading from the New Road to the Cricket Field would not be interfered with.[11]*

The footpath between the New Road (Western Road, now Manor Road) and the Cricket Club is still there.

The development of Sidmouth was continuing elsewhere:

> **03/01/1883** *The Manor Trustees have demolished some of their dilapidated cottages and have offered the land as building sites, and they have now put before the public a scheme for building a continuous and uniform terrace of handsome houses along the front of the Esplanade, so that all that is now required is speculative builders.[12]*

At the beginning of 1883, perhaps indicative of the trend away from renting whole houses, both 7 and 8 Fortfield Terrace were empty and available to let. In February, a dead pilot whale was washed up on Sidmouth beach. It was an unusual event which generated a lot of interest locally. Remarkably, at such a relatively recent time in an era of scientific curiosity, most people thought that whales were fishes, and so the local papers carried articles explaining that they were, in fact, mammals.

In July that year the lodging-houses and their proprietors were listed in *The Sidmouth Directory*: No 1, Mrs Churchill: No 2, Mrs Fitzgerald: No 3, Mrs Cartwright: No 4, Mrs Soloman: No 9, Mrs Slade. Quite a change for Fortfield Terrace in just under 100 years, from holiday homes for the wealthy to seaside lodgings.

On 19 June, 1884, *Lethaby's* records the arrival in Sidmouth of John Edward Heugh Balfour, heir to the Manor of Sidmouth, and generally considered to be the best thing that had happened to Sidmouth for many years.

> *At ten o'clock in the evening a superb display of Fireworks, gratuitously provided by Mr Balfour in the Fortfield, was witnessed by many hundreds of the inhabitants... the display itself was superior to anything of the sort ever seen in Sidmouth. Rockets and other projectiles there were in abundance, producing a charming effect as they showered their golden and coloured drops upon the sea.[13]*

He had recently celebrated his twenty-first birthday, but it was not until his twenty-fifth on 22 January, 1888 that he became Lord of the Manor. His Trustees agreed to the building of the Manor House, as for the first time Sidmouth had a resident Lord of the Manor. I think it would be true to say that he did not disappoint. He made Sidmouth his home, served in the British Army rising to the rank of Colonel, was appointed Companion of the Most Distinguished Order of Saint Michael and Saint George and was awarded the Distinguished Service Order. He made many improvements to the town and was President of the Sid Vale Association until his death in 1952.

As we saw earlier there were worldwide celebrations of Queen Victoria's 50 years as British monarch. The Fort Field was again lit up on June 20, **1887** as Sidmouth celebrated the Jubilee. A procession formed in front of Fortfield Terrace, went around the town and then back to the Cricket Field.

> *The excellent position which Fortfield Terrace offers was fully taken advantage of by the respective occupants, most particularly in the way of illuminations, which with the reflections cast over the windows, caused by coloured lights from the cricket field constituted a lovely sight.*[14]

It must have looked something like this:

FORTFIELD TERRACE ILLUMINATED
from photograph 2006

❧ DEAN PLUMPTRE ❧

Sandwiched between these celebrations and the succession of the new Lord of the Manor, the Dean of Wells and his wife spent four months between Oct 1887 and January 1888 at No 7. Edward Hayes Plumptre became Dean of Wells in 1881. He had a strong academic background and wrote several theological and literary works, and the occasional hymn, including the well-known 'Thy Hand O God Has Guided'.

The Plumptres had come to Sidmouth earlier than planned due to Mrs Plumptre's poor health. At the time, the Dean was finishing his book, *Life and Letters of Thomas Ken, Bishop of Bath and Wells*, and Sidmouth Museum has three letters written by him to the Rev Canon Moar. These refer to an original seventeenth century letter by Bishop Ken which the Canon had lent him. The Dean photographed the original and sent the photograph to his publisher. He returned the letter to the Canon by parcel post, insuring it for £5. Unfortunately, the publisher would only accept the original, so the precious document was sent back to the Dean and on to the publisher. As a token of his gratitude the Dean sent the Canon a signed note from Cardinal Manning to add to his autograph collection.

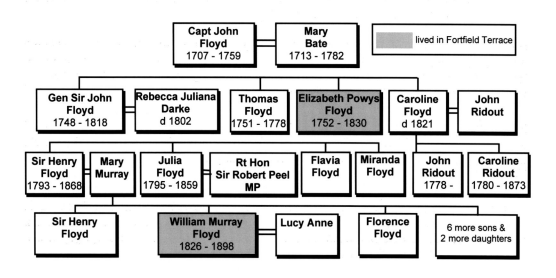

LETTER FROM DEAN PLUMPTRE TO CANON MOAR 1887
Sidmouth Museum

The book was to be Dean Plumptre's last literary work, and he died three years later at the age of 70.

❧ THE FLOYDS ❧

| | lived in Fortfield Terrace |

Capt John Floyd 1707 - 1759 — **Mary Bate** 1713 - 1782

Gen Sir John Floyd 1748 - 1818 — **Rebecca Juliana Darke** d 1802 | **Thomas Floyd** 1751 - 1778 | **Elizabeth Powys Floyd** 1752 - 1830 | **Caroline Floyd** d 1821 — **John Ridout**

Sir Henry Floyd 1793 - 1868 — **Mary Murray** | **Julia Floyd** 1795 - 1859 — **Rt Hon Sir Robert Peel MP** | **Flavia Floyd** | **Miranda Floyd** | **John Ridout** 1778 - | **Caroline Ridout** 1780 - 1873

Sir Henry Floyd | **William Murray Floyd** 1826 - 1898 — **Lucy Anne** | **Florence Floyd** | 6 more sons & 2 more daughters

This seems an appropriate moment at which to tell the story of the Floyd family. William Murray Floyd can be spotted in the 1881 census lodging at Mrs Fitzgerald's at No 2. He had his moment of fame in this decade. But the story of the Floyds and their connection with Fortfield Terrace and Sidmouth goes back to the very beginning of the Terrace. It starts in Shropshire in the eighteenth century.

Captain John Floyd (1707-1758) married Mary Bate (1713-1782). They lived in Shrewsbury and had a son, John (1748 – 1818) and two daughters, Elizabeth Powys Floyd (born 1750) and Caroline Floyd. Caroline married John Christopher Ridout in 1777, and they had a son, John in 1778, and a daughter Caroline in 1780.

On the death of Mary in 1782, Elizabeth Powys Floyd was left half the linen, plate and china, and the right to live at the family home on St John's Hill, Shrewsbury with Mary's friend, Sarah Reynolds, as long as Elizabeth was unmarried. John Floyd had the house and paid the taxes.[15] In 1795, Elizabeth became the first leaseholder of No 7 Fort Terrace, Sidmouth. She built two well-known Sidmouth houses, Witheby between 1800 and 1810, which she sold, and then Powys Cottage between 1819 and 1826. After her death, Powys passed to her nephew, Sir Henry Floyd Bart.

Elizabeth's brother John rose through the army ranks in the Dragoons, eventually becoming a general in 1812. He served in India from 1782 to 1800, and in Ireland from 1809 to 1812. He was created a Baronet in 1816. He married Rebecca Juliana Darke in Madras in 1791. They had two children, Sir Henry Floyd (1793-1868), and Julia (1795-1859) who married the Rt Hon Sir Robert Peel MP in 1820.

Sir Henry served in the army rising to the rank of Major-General in 1851. In 1821, he married Mary, eldest daughter of William Murray of Jamaica. They had eleven children - 8 boys and 3 girls. The eldest son was Sir Henry Floyd of Powys, and the second son was William Murray Floyd (born Brighton, 1826).

All we know about William Floyd's early days is that at the 1851 census, at the age of 25, he was living at Orchard Villa in Sidmouth with his unmarried first cousin once removed Caroline Ridout (born in Shrewsbury), and was recorded as working in the East India Company Service. The 1861 census showed him living with Caroline, now 80, at No 1 Eaglehurst, Sidmouth, and retired from the Bengal Civil Service. In 1871 he was living with his mother Mary (now widowed), Caroline Ridout, and his sister Florence at Powys. Caroline died two years later at the age of 92.

In March 1877 he moved into 2 Fortfield Terrace where he lodged with Mrs Fitzgerald until the end of 1884. He then disappeared from our records, and reappeared three years later, at the age of 61, married and living with his wife Lucy Ann (aged 28) at 3 Brooklet Villas, then in Salcombe Regis, but now in Sidmouth, at the bottom of Hillside Road.

He was well known and respected around town where he was on the Local Committee of the RSPCA and the Sidmouth Dispensary and was Honorary Secretary to the Sidmouth Lifeboat Institution. He was also the Local Secretary to the British Seamen's Orphan Home, Brixham.

William's moment of fame came in 1881 when on 23 May, the Duke and Duchess of Edinburgh arrived offshore aboard HMS *Lively* to inspect Sidmouth Coastguard Station. A recent article in *The Sidmouth Herald* commemorated this event (see next page), which was also documented in the RNLI Journal.

SIDMOUTH HERALD
October 14, 2005

The lifeboat was launched to greet the Duke and Duchess. The boat ferrying them ashore almost capsized in the heavy swell, and the royal party was transferred to the lifeboat. Among the lifeboat crew of ten oarsmen and steersman was William Floyd, who sat on the gunwale to make more room and promptly fell overboard. *The Sidmouth Directory and General Advertiser* reported that 'Mr Floyd was pulled into the boat in a rather exhausted condition, but as it is not the first time that he has experienced a sudden immersion, he was to some extent unconcerned'.

The following telegram was received by Mr John Barber (Chief Officer of the Sidmouth Coastguards) on the day after:

> ***Torquay, May 24, 1881 - From H S Rickard, HMS Lively, Torquay to Mr John Barber, Chief Officer, Coast Guard, Sidmouth.***
> *Duke and Duchess of Edinburgh desire you will enquire after health of Mr Floyd, and express their hope that he has felt no ill effects on account of yesterday's occurrence.*[16]

This reply was sent:

> *Mr Floyd through Mr Barber returns his grateful thanks to their Royal Highnesses for their kind recollection. He is well. Accident result of a fainting fit, through weakness. [Apparently Mr Floyd had only recently recovered from an illness.]*[16]

Lethaby's Journal records that on 16 June Mr Floyd received photos of the Duke and Duchess autographed "Alfred" on one and "Marie" on the other, and a letter:

> **Eastwell Park, Ashford, Kent 15 June 1881**
> *Dear Sir – I am desired by the Duke and Duchess of Edinburgh to request your acceptance of the enclosed photographs of Their Royal Highnesses, as a memento of their visit to Sidmouth. Their Royal Highnesses trust that you have recovered from any ill effects you may have felt from your immersion on the occasion of their landing.*
> *I am, dear Sir, yours faithfully, F H Poore, Equerry in Waiting.*[17]

Mr Floyd sent a photograph of himself in Life Boat costume to the Duchess and received this letter in reply:

> **Eastwell Park, etc. 18 June, 1881.**
> *Dear Mr Floyd – Her Royal Highness desires me to thank you very much for the photograph you have sent, which she is pleased to accept as a reminiscence of the opportune assistance rendered by yourself and the Life Boat crew, on the occasion of her landing at Sidmouth.*
> *Believe me, yours very truly, F H Poore.*[17]

In February 1897 William Floyd, in his last recorded charitable act, gave £1 to the Mansion House Indian Famine Fund. *The Sidmouth Observer And Visitors' List* of 27 July, 1898 reported his death:

> *DEATH OF MR W M FLOYD   Sidmouth has lost another valued inhabitant by the death of Mr William Murray Floyd, whose demise we regret having to record today, Although deceased lived just outside the parish boundary, viz., at No. 3, Brooklett-villas, in Salcombe-Regis, he always identified himself with, and took an active interest in, all matters, more particularly those of a philanthropic nature, connected with Sidmouth, and his death has occasioned a vacancy it will be difficult to fill. He was the second son of the late Sir Henry Floyd, Bart., who used to live at Powys. For many years deceased was the popular secretary of the Sidmouth Lifeboat Institution, and scarcely ever missed accompanying the crew on their periodical launches. Some of our readers may, perhaps, remember that on the occasion of the visit of the Duke and Duchess of Edinburgh in their yacht to Sidmouth, he accompanied the crew to meet the distinguished visitors, and on returning had the misfortune to fall overboard, but happily with no ill-consequences, a touch of humour being given to the mishap by his subsequent apology to the Duchess for his abrupt leave of absence. He was a never failing friend to the fishermen, and they will especially regret his loss. We may mention that it was due to his efforts that the Beacon Lamp was established on the Esplanade, this having proved a most useful adjunct to the fishermen in the pursuit of their calling. His sympathy and support was also given to the 'Sid Vale' Court of Foresters, and, as the hon. sec. of the Sidmouth Band of Mercy he did all in his power to obtain kind and considerate treatment for dumb animals from their owners. He likewise associated himself with other local institutions, and was always a ready and willing helper if anything deserving [sic] notice. He passed peacefully away to his rest on Friday, at the age of 72, after an illness extending over several weeks. The funeral will take place today, at noon, at Salcombe.*[18]

and a week later, his funeral:

> *The funeral of Mr W M Floyd, whose death we recorded last week, took place on Wednesday last, in the little churchyard at Salcombe. The coffin, of polished oak, bore the following inscription: 'William Murray Floyd, died 22nd July, 1898, aged 72 years.' It was borne to the grave by members of the Lifeboat crew. The Rev W J Baugh officiated. There were many mourners present, and a large number of beautiful wreaths, &c., were placed upon the grave, including one from the fishermen and another from the Foresters. During the service at Salcombe, a muffled peal was rung upon the bells of Sidmouth Church.[19]*

WILLIAM FLOYD
by Col Hawker
Sidmouth Museum

It seems to have been a fitting tribute to a good man, who in *Lethaby's Journal* of 1 September, 1881 was described rather movingly as 'that warm friend of the forlorn'.

CHAPTER FOURTEEN
1890 - 1899

&ca; TOWARDS THE NEXT CENTURY &ca;

1890 - 1899

In **1890** the British Empire in Africa expanded by the allocation of various African countries between Britain, Germany, Portugal and France by a number of treaties. 1890 also proved a landmark year for women: Flora Lugard became the first female foreign correspondent of *The Times*, and Philippa Fawcett achieved top marks in mathematics at Cambridge, although unfortunately she was not eligible to be awarded a degree. In **1891** Arthur Conan Doyle's *The Adventures of Sherlock Holmes* was published in *The Strand* magazine. **1892** saw the death of Alfred, Lord Tennyson. **1893** was a significant year in technology in which Karl Benz in Germany and Henry Ford in the USA produced their first motor-cars, Alexander Graham Bell made the first long-distance telephone call, and most importantly, Whitcome Judson patented the zip-fastener. **1894** saw the resignation of Gladstone at the end of his fourth term as Prime Minister, and the opening of Tower Bridge, Blackpool Tower and the Manchester Ship Canal.

By the end of **1895** the world had seen the discovery of Xrays, the first radio broadcast by Marconi, the first moving cinematography and Oscar Wilde's *The Importance of Being Earnest*. In a time of looking into the future, it was recognised that the past should not be forgotten, and The National Trust was founded that year. In a risky move, in **1896** the speed limit was raised from 4mph plus man with red flag, to 20mph. The shape of things to come was established in **1897** with the first conviction for drink driving and the first motoring fatality on Britain's roads, a nine year old boy killed by a taxi. This was also the year of Queen Victoria's Diamond Jubilee. In **1898** Gladstone died, Kitchener imposed order in the Sudan with victory at Omdurman, and H G Wells wrote *The War of The Worlds*. The end of an extraordinary decade at the end of an amazing century was marked by the start of the Second Anglo-Boer War in **1899**, with Ladysmith, Kimberley and Mafeking becoming household names. The British Empire had become the largest the world had ever known, covering one fifth of the total land mass of the planet, and one quarter of the world's population.

❧ MEANWHILE, BACK IN SIDMOUTH ❧

By the beginning of the 1890s, just about 100 years after it was built, much of Fortfield Terrace was run as lodging-houses, with the lodging-house keepers being tenants of the Manor Estate.

No 1	*Mr and Mrs Lake*	*No 4*	*Mrs Soloman*
No 2	*Mrs Fitzgerald*	*No 7*	*Mrs Pile*
No 3	*Mrs Cartwright*	*Nos 9 and 10*	*Mrs Slade*

Nos 1½, 5, 6 and 8 were still being let on behalf of the Manor Estate as single houses.

Advertisements appeared on behalf of both groups:

```
Furnished Apartments - Pile, Mrs. 7 Fortfield Terrace.
          Facing the Cricket Ground and Sea.
```

```
TO BE LET furnished No 6 Fortfield Terrace. Apply to
     Radford and Orchard, Solicitors, Sidmouth
```

❧ THE GREAT WATER DEBATE ❧

Progress, in the form of reservoir water supply, was being resisted by those who wanted to continue using their own well water. There were vested interests: the newly formed Water Company wanted to sell a commodity which many considered their traditional right.

So in 1891 there was a heated exchange of correspondence in *The Sidmouth Observer and Visitors' List* between two of the town's doctors on the subject of the quality of the well water at No 8 Fortfield Terrace. Dr Williams started it by saying that some visitors to the Terrace and one of the servants at No 8 had become ill through drinking contaminated well water.

Dr Pullin responded vigorously:

> *CORRESPONDENCE – on The Water Supply of Sidmouth. Sir, - The suggested proof of the impurity of the well of No 8, Fortfield Terrace, by Dr Williams, in your issue of yesterday, is not a happy one. In the first instance, the family and servants look on it in the light of a breach of professional confidence, and secondly, the patient states that she has never enjoyed better health than since her service at No 8, and is able to appeal to my own professional knowledge of her from birth, in verification of her statement. Was it ever intimated to the patient that sewage polluted water was the supposed cause of her indisposition? She herself says emphatically "NO". Yours obliged, Thos. H.S.Pullin, Medical Officer of Health. January 1, 1891.* [1]

Dr Williams decided to get personal:

> *CORRESPONDENCE – on The Water Supply of Sidmouth. Dear Sir, -*
> *Finally, let me say that I did not instance the health of an inmate as*
> *suggesting a proof of the impurity of the well water at 8, Fortfield Terrace.*
> *That impurity has already been amply proved by the analysis and report*
> *of Mr Perkins, whose position as Public Analyst at Exeter is a sufficient*
> *guarantee of his accuracy. This gentleman has furnished me with two*
> *reports on well-water, one at 9 Fortfield Terrace, the other in Russell*
> *Street, with regard to which it is instructive to note; 1, that among the*
> *consumers there have, in each case, been two deaths from Diphtheria;*
> *2, that in each case the deceased persons were either visitors or recent*
> *comers to Sidmouth; 3, that the well water in each case was found*
> *polluted with sewage; 4, that in each case, Dr Pullin 'tested the water,*
> *and would have no hesitation in drinking it himself'. Yours faithfully,*
> *Leonard Williams January 12, 1891.*[2]

The exchange fortunately petered out at this stage, with a rather restrained letter from Dr Pullin. I suspect they both realised that this debate was not in the interests of good business.

> *CORRESPONDENCE – on The Water Supply of Sidmouth. In connec-*
> *tion with the first cases of illness in strangers at Fortfield-terrace, I have*
> *shewn that the adjoining large household of residents, of from 12 to 15*
> *inmates, used during the illness and are still using, from the same well,*
> *without the slightest apparent ill effect. Thos. H.S.Pullin.*[3]

Progress was not to be resisted and I am not aware of any households in Fortfield Terrace currently using well water, though the Sidmouth Cricket, Tennis, Hockey and Croquet Club has recently bucked the trend by using water from a bore-hole to water the pitches.

The 1891 Census of April 5 looked like this:

1	William Lake	Head	M	48	Lodging House Keeper	Exeter
	Elizabeth Lake	Wife	M	42		Handworth
	Edward Lake	Son		12	Scholar	Sidmouth
	Annie Lake	Daughter		8	Scholar	Honiton
	Lavinia Prewer	Servant	S	22	General Servant	Honiton
	Elizabeth Blackman	Head	W	63	Living on means	Cambridge
	Alfred Blackman	Son	S	21	Living on means	Whitstable
	Agnes Blackman	Daughter	S	26	Living on means	Whitstable
	Alice Blackman	Daughter	S	24	Living on means	Whitstable
	Adelaide Bolton	Lodger	S	62	Living on means	Southsea
1 ½	Catherine Blake	Head	S	72	Living on means	Ireland
	Sarah A Hoskins	Servant	S	49	Parlour Maid	Sidmouth
	Jessie Holmes	Servant	S	43	Cook	Sidmouth
2	Mary Fitzgerald	Head	W	52	Lodging House Keeper	Sidmouth
	Mary A Fitzgerald	Daughter	S	22	Help Domestic	Sidmouth
	Thomas E Fitzgerald	Son		13	Scholar	Sidmouth
	Emily Thomas	Servant	S	19	General Servant	Colyton
	Anthony Thorold	Head	W	65	Bishop of Winchester	Haigham, Lincs
	Dorothy M Thorold	Daughter	S	18		St Pancras, London
	Sybil E Thorold	Daughter	S	16		St Pancras London
	Agnes F A Ricoffi	Servant	S	63	Governess	Wurtemburg
	George Clark	Servant	S	28	Butler	Stratford on Avon
	Margaret Taylor	Lodger	S	43	Living on means	Cupar, Fife
	Graham F Ross	Nephew		12		Glasgow
	Barbara A Pesel	Visitor	W	43	Living on means	South Australia
	Florence Pesel	Visitor	S	21	Living on means	Huddersfield

	Name	Relation		Age	Occupation	Birthplace
3	Harriet Cartwright	Head	W	69	Lodging House Keeper	Salcombe Regis
	Emily Cartwright	Daughter	S	38	Assistant	St Pauls, Bristol
	Rosa Savage	Head	W	68	Living on means	Dublin
	Sarah Keogh	Servant	S	45	Lady's Maid	Co. Wicklow
4	Elizabeth Soloman	Head	M	59	Lodging House Keeper	Sidmouth
	Sarah J Harrison	Visitor	S	30	Children's Nurse	Newton Le Willows
	Ronald D Langton	Visitor		7		Cromton, Lancs
	Gertrude D Langton	Visitor		5		Cromton, Lancs
	Amy Carslake	Servant	S	22	General Servant	Sidbury
	Lucy S Pattison	Lodger	W	40	Living on means	USA
	Elizabeth Johnson	Lodger	S	59	Living on means	USA
5	William Martin	Head	W	90	Living on means	Ireland
	Lucretia A Martin	Daughter	S	59	Living on means	Ireland
	Annie Gill	Companion	S	27		Helston
	Mary Page	Servant	S	33	Cook Domestic Servant	Sidmouth
	Emma Way	Servant	S	27	Housemaid	Ottery St Mary
7	Allan Pile	Head	M	34	Gardener	Sidmouth
	Alice Pile	Wife	M	28	Lodging House Keeper	Bromham, Wilts
	Arthur J Pile	Son		7	Scholar	Sidmouth
	Allan C Pile	Son		5	Scholar	Sidmouth
	Alice Pile	Daughter		1m		Sidmouth
	Ann Davis	M in Law	M	60	Nurse domestic	Bromham, Wilts
	Susan Banfield	Servant	S	22	General Servant	Sidbury
	Katharine Fletcher	Head	M	26	Living on means	Oxford
	Leslie Fletcher	Son		5		Oxford
	George Fletcher	Son		3		Oxford
	Charlotte M Taywill	Visitor	W	49	Living on means	Hornsey, Middlesex
	Susannah Johnson	Servant	S	39	Nurse Domestic Servant	North Creake, Norfolk
	Ruth Gibbard	Servant	S	19	Nurse Domestic Servant	Ardley, Oxfordshire
	Charles Rhodes	Head	M	50	Congregational Minister	Morley, Yorks
	Alice G Rhodes	Wife	M	44		Burton in Lonsdale
8	Douglas Bolton	Head	M	57	Col HM Land Forces	Tipperary, Ireland
	Fanny Bolton	Wife	M	49		Dharwar, India
	Evelyn Bolton	Daughter	S	17		Sidmouth
	Mary Bolton	Daughter	S	16		Bombay, India
	Shane Bolton	Son		14		Kurralhee, India
	Lilian Bolton	Daughter		12		Sidmouth
	Elizabeth Mutters	Servant	S	47	Nurse Domestic	Sidbury
	Ela Wells	Servant	S	32	Cook	Kelly, Devon
	Louisa Garwood	Servant	S	18	Housemaid	Exmouth
9&10	Elizabeth Slade	Head	W	49	Lodging House Keeper	Bromham, Wilts
	Edith Howard	Servant	S	15	General Servant	Sidmouth
	Sarah Page	Servant	S	17	General Servant	Sidmouth
	Sarah A Hart	Lodger		67	Living on means	Middlesex
	Heber L Hart	Lodger		26	Barrister at Law	Stockwell, Surrey
	Sarah S Hart	Lodger		27	Proprietresses of school	Stockwell, Surrey
	Ada L Hart	Lodger		30		Stockwell, Surrey
	Henry E Roberts	Head		38	Curate of Sidmouth	St Pauls, London
	Beatrice L Roberts	Wife		26	Parish Church	Ireland
	Basil C Roberts	Son		3		Cheltenham
	Gwenllian R Foster	Servant		17	Nursemaid	Cheltenham
	Anna C Samuells	Head		68	Living on means	Bengal, India
	Mary E Samuells	Daughter		42	Living on means	Edinburgh
	Margaret P Samuells	Daughter		30	Living on means	Middlesex

Even though No 6 was empty, there were eighty residents in the Terrace that night. It was a good night to be in the Terrace: not only was Rt Rev Anthony Thorold, the Bishop of Winchester, staying at Mrs Fitzgerald's, but the Congregational Minister, Rev Charles Rhodes was at Mrs Pile's and the Curate of the Parish Church, Rev Henry Roberts, was at Mrs Slade's. For more earthly needs there were the usual collection of army personnel, lawyers and teachers, not to mention a small army of servants.

It is likely that there was a change of proprietor at Nos 9 and 10 at the end of the year, as this advertisement appeared and the house was empty for four months.

These were times when almost anything seemed possible. A lecture was held in Sidmouth in April 1891 on the possibility of building a Tunnel under the English Channel connecting England and France. During that year the Manor Hall (Manor Pavilion), Sidmouth's still thriving theatre, opened its doors for the first time. It contained the offices of the celebrated architect R W Sampson, who moved to Sidmouth in 1891, and whose designs over the next four decades were to have a major impact on Sidmouth.[4] Just up the road (Western Road in those days), the Red House (later to become the Fortfield Hotel) was being built. The following year Mr J Leese QC MP and his family moved in.

In July 1892 Col Douglas Bolton of No 8 died.

Death on July 15th, at 8, Fortfield Terrace of Col J S D Bolton, Bombay Staff Corps, fourth son of Colonel John Bolton, late of 75th and 67th Regiments Native Infantry, also late Poor Law Commissioner, Fermoy, Ireland. Obituary: Died at the age of 58 after a month's illness. Son of Lieut-Colonel John Bolton who joined the 67th Regiment in 1813 and was afterwards a Government Poor Law Inspector at Fermoy in Ireland and died in Sidmouth in 1861. JSDB joined the Indian Army in 1851. Last public appointment in India was as cantonment magistrate at Poona. His Uncle Capt A Bolton RN was on board the Victory with Nelson at the Battle of Trafalgar. His cousin, Capt C Bolton RN married Lord Nelson's eldest sister. His uncle, General Daniel Bolton, served under the Duke of Wellington. One or other members of his family have been residents of Sidmouth during the past 40 years, and many have died here. The late Colonel leaves a widow and large family, seven sons and five daughters, all comparatively young.[5]

His funeral was reported the following week

Funeral of Colonel Bolton – The funeral took place at the cemetery on Wednesday last at one o'clock. The mournful cortege, consisting of an open funeral car and three coaches, left Fortfield Terrace shortly after half-past twelve, and slowly wended its way to the cemetery via Old Fore Street and High Street.[6]

And the following month the family left.

Sale of Household Furniture and Effects at 8, Fortfield Terrace, on Tuesday, September 27th. Messrs Pidsley and Son are instructed by the Executors of the late Col J S D Bolton, to sell as above. For particulars see posters, which will shortly be printed.[7]

At the end of 1892 Western Road became Manor Road. Shortly after that proposals were made to replace the footpath behind the Manor Hall with a carriage drive for reasons of aesthetics and convenience:

*Such drive to be dedicated to the public, both for walking and for vehicles.
This would enable coaches to turn more easily and would 'shut out from
view the ugly backs of Fortfield-terrace, and make the place more tidy
and agreeable to the sight, the ground referred to now being in a very
untidy condition'.* [8]

These proposals were obviously not carried through as the footpath is still there.

On the subject of roads, in 1893 it was noted that the road in front of Fortfield Terrace was
in bad condition, so much so that Mr Lake was refusing to send his omnibus up the
Terrace. The Local Board asked the Manor, whose responsibility it was, to repair it. A year
later:

*LOCAL BOARD Proposed path to railway station. Request to Capt
Balfour to give 10 feet of land from the Esplanade to Fortfield-Terrace,
and a portion of the land now occupied by the wall at the East end of the
terrace so as to make a footpath of suitable width. The Board would
undertake to rebuild and fence the wall along the cricket field and along
the East end of the terrace.* [9]

The following year, the road at the front of the Terrace was repaired at the cost of £80 to
the Local Board, prompting outrage that public money had been spent on a private road.
Where would we be today without a bit of mutual back-scratching?

The seasonal nature of the holiday trade was commented on in *The Sidmouth Directory*:

*The Sidmouth season has once more come and gone, a fact that is easily
understood by the number of boards, worded, 'Apartments to let', that
may be seen outside many of our lodging-houses. Nearly all holiday-
makers and tourists are now, possibly, engaged in occupations of a less
agreeable nature than climbing the hills of picturesque Devon; and we
are left with those comparatively few visitors who prefer to take their
holidays at a time when the autumn tints may be seen in their beauty.* [10]

Perhaps those few visitors would have been further encouraged by the flotation of the
Sidmouth Baths Company Ltd in November 1893, and the opening of The Sidmouth Brine
Baths in 1895.

A happy event was reported on 21 March, 1894:

*A very pretty wedding took place at the Wesleyan Chapel on Monday, the
contracting parties being Mr George House of Brankscombe, and Miss
Edith, third daughter of Mr Mills, of Fortfield terrace, Sidmouth [The new
lodging-house keeper of No 9]. The bride was very prettily attired, and
attended by three bridesmaids, Miss K Mills (of Clifton), cousin, Misses
Minnie and Alice Mills (sisters), who were arrayed in becoming costumes.
The newly-married pair left the Chapel amid a heavy shower of rice, and
with the good wishes of a large circle of friends.* [11]

The new Sidmouth Urban District Council had its first meeting in January 1895. High on
the agenda was the proposal that Sidmouth should annex Sidbury and parts of Salcombe
Regis. Not surprisingly it was reported that there was 'vigorous opposition' from Salcombe
Regis and Sidbury, but all to no avail.

Following on from the health issues raised by the well water debate, canine concerns surfaced again about the number of dogs in Sidmouth in a letter entitled 'The Dog Nuisance' caused by 'the plethora of dogs in Sidmouth'. Generally dogs and drains greatly exercised the minds of the people of Sidmouth. With regard to the latter, the occupier of No 6 applied to the Council for a certificate as to the sanitary condition of the premises.

> *On the motion of Mr Skinner, seconded by Mr Millen, it was resolved that the Surveyor and Inspector of Nuisances visit the house in question, and, if satisfied with its sanitary condition, grant the certificate.*[12]

The surveyor reported back:

> *With regard to giving a certificate for No 6 Fortfield-terrace, we, ie both Mr Wilson and myself, feel a little reticent about giving this, as we have no means of testing the drains other than by mere observation.*

> *With regard to the certificate to 6, Fortfield-terrace, the Chairman suggested that a smoke-tester should be borrowed for that house, as perhaps the not granting of the certificate might give rise to a wrong impression. It was most important that it should be known that the reason for not granting the certificate was because the Officials of the Council had not the means of testing.*[13]

The happy outcome was that the Council bought a smoke-testing machine for £6 6s, No 6's drains were declared sanitary, and the certificate was issued. It was probably coincidence that two weeks later the following advertisement appeared in the Sidmouth Directory:

```
FOR SALE, about 40 loads of good Garden mould.
         Apply to 6 Fortfield-terrace.
```

While all this was going on, a new sewerage system was under construction in Western Town. It was completed in 1897 and was commended in no less a publication than *The British Medical Journal*. The new sewerage system is still operational, but is no longer new (and only just operational).

It was probably also coincidence that around this time the following death was reported:

> *We regret to record the death of Mr Charles Edward Peake, of Sleaford, Lincolnshire, which occurred at 6, Fortfield-terrace, Sidmouth, on the 3rd instant. Deceased, who was an invalid, and came here for the benefit of his health a considerable time ago, was 39 years of age.*[14]

Although much had changed over the years, people still had faith in the healing powers of Sidmouth's air; and probably also in the efficacy of Dr Tibbles Vi-Cocoa which 'Gives power to the involuntary muscles of the body. And, way ahead of its time, it put forward the idea that, 'as people become more intelligent, they see that they should try and *prevent* disease.' Case studies were presented:

VI-COCOA ADVERTISEMENTS
Sidmouth Directory and General Advertiser   Sidmouth Museum

Of many claims for its efficacy, I find this the most compelling. I must leave you to come to your own conclusion as to the interpretation of this statement:

VI-COCOA LEADS THE WAY.	It is found in the Homes of Hundreds of Thousands of the People who cannot be induced to go without it.

Where the sea air, preventive measures, and Vi-Cocoa were ineffective, one could always turn to Dr Williams' Pink Pills for Pale People.

DR WILLIAMS' PINK PILLS ADVERTISEMENTS
Sidmouth Directory and General Advertiser   Sidmouth Museum

Evidence proves the undoubted cure by Dr Williams' Pink Pills for Pale People of the following: Anaemia, Rickets, Pale and Sallow Complexion, Loss of Vital Forces, Scrofula and Hysteria.

As time went by, 'Fatal diseases' was added to the list.

Again, the advertisers were way ahead of their time in the promotion of evidence-based medicine, though all the evidence was anecdotal.

There were more fireworks in 1897. Firstly, in March, there was a violent storm, which caused damage in the Terrace:

> *TERRIFIC GALE LAST NIGHT – Great Damage Done... at No 1, Fort-field-terrace, the damage is more serious still, and the occupants have had a miraculous escape from injury. The upper portion of the back part of the house has been entirely demolished. The chimney fell early this morning, sending the roof into the bedroom (which had been occupied shortly before) and taking the side of the house into the roadway.*[15]

Secondly, June marked the Diamond Jubilee of Queen Victoria's reign on the 22nd:

> *On the decorations, Nos 1, 1 ½, 8, 9 and 10 of Fortfield-terrace, seen from the Esplanade, deserve mention.*[16]

1897 also saw the death of Peter Orlando Hutchinson, Sidmouth's own historian.

> *DEATH OF MR P O HUTCHINSON Born 17 November 1810, died 1 October 1897. He was unmarried. The funeral took place at the Sidmouth cemetery yesterday afternoon, deceased being laid to rest in a grave close to that of the late Mr William Trump.*[17]

✌ A GOOD EDUCATION ✍

The Victorians recognised the value of a good education, and for those who could afford it, a good *private* education.

Small boys could be accommodated at No 5:

```
TUITION, Classical and Modern, either Privately
              or in Class.
     ELEMENTARY CLASS FOR LITTLE BOYS.
  Leonard Morgan-Brown (Late Scholar of Corpus
            Christi College, Oxford)
         5, Fortfield-terrace, Sidmouth
```

Or bigger boys at Cambridge Terrace:

```
    Mr Rudolph Rosenstock, M.A., Oxon. (Honours)
   8 Cambridge Terrace, Sidmouth   Prepares Pupils for
    Public Schools and Universities; the Preliminary
  Examinations in Law and Medicine; Army Entrance and
  Naval Cadetships.  Special care devoted to young and
    delicate boys. Private Lessons in German can be
            arranged. HIGHEST REFERENCES.
```

Or boarding boys a bit further afield:

> The Rev E B Brutton MA   Late Scholar of Jesus College,
> Cambridge (Classical Honours) takes pupils at Aylesbeare
> Vicarage, near Exeter, to prepare for the Public
> Schools, Army Prelim, Ec., Special advantages to
> delicate or backward boys, and to those leaving home for
> the first time. Small classes. Individual attention.
> Athletics greatly encouraged. The house is very
> healthily situated on high ground, about five miles from
> Sidmouth and three miles from Broadclyst Station. Next
> term commences September 23rd .

The Rev E B Brutton MA was a keen cricketer, who spent his summer holidays at Fortfield Terrace playing cricket. In mid-August 1895 he scored 90 runs for Devon against the MCC at Exeter.

Unfortunately girls do not seem to have been particularly well provided for, but people of a more musical nature could have banjo lessons with Mr Harry Angel on a Thursday, or violin lessons with Mr Hart.

For those not academically inclined, potentially profitable mental stimulation was available just by the market place:

> *GUESSING COMPETITION   The second guessing competition ar-*
> *ranged by Mr A E Buxton, of the Public Benefit Boot Supply, New-street,*
> *has resulted in William Dale and T. Gorman gaining the prizes. Compet-*
> *itors had to guess the number of pairs of small shoes contained in a large*
> *boot. The number was 15, but no one guessed correctly, the nearest*
> *being Dale 14 and Gorman 16. They have been awarded a pair of*
> *slippers each. This week competitors have to tell the number of boots*
> *there are in a box in the window.*[18]

✃ CRIME & PUNISHMENT ✃

Education certainly wasn't on the agenda for working class girls, many of whom ended up in service, possibly responding to this sort of advertisement in *The Sidmouth Directory* on 10 July, 1895:

> Good general servant wanted: 20 - 21.
> Apply 4 Fortfield-terrace

Some were much younger than this, as in the case of Elizabeth Cooper, age 14, who worked as a domestic servant for Mrs Page, the lodging-house keeper of No 5 Fortfield Terrace. The case was reported in detail in *The Sidmouth Directory*[19] under the title 'Larceny By A Servant'. Mrs Augusta Kingsbury and her daughter, Mrs Meyer, stayed at Mrs Page's for a month in May and June 1898.

Money disappeared from Mrs Meyer's purse, and Mrs Kingsbury noticed the disappearance of:

> a knife, pair of gloves, six blank cheques on the London and County Bank at Dorking, a gold chain, three handkerchiefs, a pair of scissors, and a quantity of notepaper and envelopes.

These were found by Mrs Page in Elizabeth Cooper's box. When confronted Elizabeth began to cry. Her mother in Newton Poppleford was informed and came and took her away. The case came to court in Ottery St Mary on 7 June, 1898. Mr E J Brutton, solicitor (and possibly brother of the Rev E B Brutton, cricketer) represented Elizabeth, who pleaded guilty.

Mr Brutton then spoke on her behalf.

> Unfortunately, the girl, was one of a family who were more or less of dull intellect. The father and mother appeared to be alright, but there was this deficiency about the family, which consisted of five children. He knew for a fact that at school they were a great trouble, it being very difficult to get them to learn anything. He hoped the defendant now realised the enormity of the offence which she had committed. The father and mother had talked to her about it, and he (Mr. Brutton) had spoken to her on its seriousness that morning.

He gave the opinion that a custodial sentence would be in no-one's best interest. Had she been a boy a good flogging would probably have had 'a beneficial effect'. He asked that as it was a first offence, the Bench might consider returning her to the care of her mother, and if they decided to inflict a fine he trusted it would be such a one as the mother could pay. The magistrates decided on leniency and inflicted a fine of £1 7s, or in default of this, 14 days imprisonment.

The hearing came to a somewhat abrupt and unusual end:

> The defendant was then charged with stealing a pocket handkerchief and pair of gloves, the property of Mary Page. The Prosecutrix consented to withdraw the charge on the defendant paying the costs, 3/6. The mother said she was unable to do so. Mr Brutton, however, said he would pay the money, as he was anxious to get away. The charge was then withdrawn.

One gets the impression that considerable compassion was exercised by all concerned.

END OF A CENTURY

Fortfield Terrace and Sidmouth had come a long way in the last 100 years. In 1897 the local telephone exchange already had 20 customers, who were however limited to talking only to each other on the telephone. The comment associated with this seems somehow very appropriate to Sidmouth generally:

> There is now the prospect of connecting with the outside world if more subscribers can be found.[20]

CHAPTER FIFTEEN
1900 - 1901

❧ THE END OF THE VICTORIAN ERA ❧

1900 - 1901

At the beginning of **1900** there was a dispute about when the new century begins. For reasons unknown this subject has to be argued about every hundred years. The second Boer War continued. In China the Boxer Rebellion reached its peak. Also in 1900 the Paris World Exposition opened and Winston Churchill was elected to parliament. And, ushering in the age of another sort of world conquest, Coca-Cola went on sale in Britain for the first time.

On January, 1 **1901 t**he world celebrated the beginning of the twentieth century (to my mind a year late) and the Commonwealth of Australia was formed. On January 22 Queen Victoria died at the age of 81, having reigned for almost 64 years, longer than any other British monarch.

Judging by the newspapers of the time, even Sidmouth could not escape the national atmosphere of gloom about the Boer War, fortunately lifted by the relief of Ladysmith, then of Mafeking.

In May 1900 Three-cornered Plot (subsequently Sidmouth Triangle and now once more Three-Cornered Plot) was enclosed for the first time, and in June the Red House was advertised for auction. It failed to sell and was put up for private sale. It was later to become the Fortfield Hotel.

Fortfield Terrace folk had their own gloom to contend with. In September Mr Mills, the lodging-house keeper at No 9 died at the age of 59. You may remember that only seven years previously the Terrace had been celebrating the marriage of his daughter Edith.

Then there was the accident to Miss Northey in November, reported in *The Sidmouth Observer and Visitors' List:*

> *The accident which befell Miss Northey (of the Old Chancel) last week will, it is hoped, lead to steps being taken to place a more efficient light at the corner of Fortfield-terrace. The place where the accident occurred is positively dangerous and it is surprising that accidents do not occur there more frequently. Either the place should be better lighted or a railing placed along the highest part.*
>
> *On the evening of the 20th she was going to put a letter in the wall-box there just before 7 o'clock, when in the darkness, she walked onto the approach to the terrace and fell over into the road below. No bones were broken, but she was badly bruised and suffered much from shock.*[1]

The death of Queen Victoria on January 22, 1901 marked the end of an era which had seen amazing changes in the world, Sidmouth and Fortfield Terrace. On that day, the following people were staying in Fortfield Terrace:

1	1 1/2	2	3	4	5	6	7	8	9	10
Col and Mrs Page-Henderson Mr Durant	Miss Blake	Mr and Mrs W H Dunsmure and fam	Mrs Bree	Miss Cox	Mrs Morant and fam	Mrs Foley and fam	Mrs and Misses Werner	Mr and Mrs Gray and fam	Mr and Mrs Hall	Dr Gordon

Only Miss Blake at No 1½ provides a connection back to pre-Victorian days as the companion of Caroline Copleston. Just over a century before, the Terrace had been occupied by, if not landed gentry, certainly people of means. Now all of the houses except No 1½ and No 8 were lodging-houses. Sidmouth as a seaside town had changed, reflecting a general change in society, but it had still managed to maintain its elegant character.

Fortfield Terrace could now be sent home as a postcard – 'weather is lovely, wish you were here'.

FORTFIELD TERRACE postcard by F Frith and Co 1904

❧ EPILOGUE ❧

For all the change that had already taken place, few could have envisaged the events and changes that the twentieth century would bring. For Fortfield Terrace it involved the selling off of the Terrace to its tenants, and the conversion of some of the houses into hotels, and then into apartments. Through it all Sidmouth and Fortfield Terrace have retained their charm and remain to this day a very pleasant place in which to live, to spend a holiday or just to be.

LIST OF ILLUSTRATIONS

REFERENCES

FOREWORD
1   **A DESCRIPTIVE SKETCH OF SIDMOUTH** comprising its ancient and modern history *by Theodore H Mogridge Esq, Member of the Royal College of Surgeons* Rose Cottage, Sidmouth 1836
2   **A POETIC CHRONICLER WITHOUT PEER; BETJEMAN'S BRITAIN** Selected, edited and introduced *by Candida Lycett Green* The Folio Society 1999
3   **STILL SIDMOUTH** *John Betjeman* Peretti Publishing, Ottery St Mary 2000
4   **THE CENTURY MAKERS – 1952** *Matthew Sturgis* Daily Telegraph London 29/11/2003
5   **HISTORIC SIDMOUTH: LIFE AND TIMES IN SIDMOUTH : A GUIDE TO THE BLUE PLAQUES** *Julia Creeke* Sid Vale Association 1992

PROLOGUE
1   **THE SIDMOUTH DIRECTORY AND GENERAL ADVERTISER** printed and published by Charles Culverwell, Fore Street, Sidmouth   December 4, 1882

CHAPTER 1 – ITALIAN BEGINNINGS
1   **M2 PRESSWIRE** August 7, 2003
2   **SIDMOUTH: A HISTORY** (p.46) *ed. Geoffrey Holmes* Sidmouth Museum 1987
3   **A HISTORY OF THE TOWN, PARISH AND MANOR OF SIDMOUTH VOL III** *Peter Orlando Hutchinson* 1880
4   **ANNA MARIA JENKINS: WILLIAM JENKINS** National Portrait Gallery
5   **A HISTORY OF THE TOWN, PARISH AND MANOR OF SIDMOUTH VOL III** *Peter Orlando Hutchinson* 1880
6   **A STORY OF SIDMOUTH** (p.23) *Anna Sutton*   James Townsend & Sons Ltd, Exeter 1959

CHAPTER 2 – HOLIDAY HOMES BY THE SEA
1   **DANDIES – A Series of 50 Cigarette Cards** John Player & Sons 1932
2   **THE ENGLISH SEASIDE RESORT: A SOCIAL HISTORY 1750-1914** (p.49) *John K Walton* Leicester University Press 1983
3   **HISTORIC SIDMOUTH: LIFE AND TIMES IN SIDMOUTH : A GUIDE TO THE BLUE PLAQUES** *Julia Creeke* Sid Vale Association 1992
4   **TREWMAN'S EXETER FLYING POST** March 14, 1787
5   **A HISTORY OF THE TOWN, PARISH AND MANOR OF SIDMOUTH VOL III** *Peter Orlando Hutchinson* 1880

CHAPTER 3 – GEORGIAN ELEGANCE
1   **A PORTRAIT OF JANE AUSTEN** *David Cecil* Book Club Associates 1978
2   **SANDITON AND OTHER STORIES** *Jane Austen Ed. Peter Washington* Everyman's Library, 1996
3   **LETHABY'S SIDMOUTH JOURNAL AND DIRECTORY** printed and published by Richard Lethaby, Market Place, Sidmouth April 1, 1864
4   **THE ENGLISH SEASIDE RESORT: A SOCIAL HISTORY 1750-1914** (p.114) *John K Walton* Leicester University Press 1983
5   **TREWMAN'S EXETER FLYING POST** May 29, 1806

CHAPTER 4 – REGENCY DAYS
1   **DANDIES – A Series of 50 Cigarette Cards** John Player & Sons 1932
2   **A HISTORY OF THE TOWN, PARISH AND MANOR OF SIDMOUTH VOL III** *Peter Orlando Hutchinson* 1880
3   **A HISTORY OF THE TOWN, PARISH AND MANOR OF SIDMOUTH VOL III** *Peter Orlando Hutchinson* 1880
4   **THE BEAUTIES OF SIDMOUTH DISPLAYED 3rd Ed** *the Rev. Edmund Butcher* printed for John Wallis proprietor of the Royal Marine Library 1820
5   **TREWMAN'S EXETER FLYING POST** January 1, 1818

CHAPTER 5 – THE GEORGIAN FINALE

1   **THE ENGLISH SEASIDE RESORT: A SOCIAL HISTORY 1750-1914** (p.77) *John K Walton* Leicester University Press 1983
2   **A HISTORY OF THE TOWN, PARISH AND MANOR OF SIDMOUTH VOL III** *Peter Orlando Hutchinson* 1880
3   **THE LETTERS OF EDWARD COPLESTON, BISHOP OF LLANDAFF, 1828-1849** *ed. Roger Lee Brown* Cardiff: South Wales Record Society 2003
4   **MEMOIR OF EDWARD COPLESTON DD, BISHOP OF LLANDAFF** William James Copleston John W Parker & Son, London 1851
5   *ibid.*
6   **UNPUBLISHED LETTERS** *Edward Copleston* Beinecke Rare Book and Manuscript Library, Yale University Library
7   **THE LETTERS OF EDWARD COPLESTON, BISHOP OF LLANDAFF, 1828-1849** *ed. Roger Lee Brown* Cardiff: South Wales Record Society 2003
8   **ibid.**
9   **ibid.**
10   **UNPUBLISHED LETTERS** *Edward Copleston* Beinecke Rare Book and Manuscript Library, Yale University Library
11   **THE LETTERS OF EDWARD COPLESTON, BISHOP OF LLANDAFF, 1828-1849** *ed. Roger Lee Brown* Cardiff: South Wales Record Society 2003
12   **LETHABY'S SIDMOUTH JOURNAL AND DIRECTORY** printed and published by Richard Lethaby, Market Place, Sidmouth October 1, 1880
13   **SIDMOUTH CHRONICLES** *John Tindall* August 14, 1914
14   **THE LIFE AND TIMES OF GEORGE IV** *Alan Palmer* Book Club Associates, London 1972

CHAPTER 6 - A ROYAL RUSSIAN VISIT

1   **FREE ARTIST: THE STORY OF ANTON AND NICHOLAS RUBINSTEIN** *Catherine Drinker Bowen* Random House, New York 1939
2   **ibid.**
3   cited in **TSAR NICHOLAS I** *Constantin de Grunwald trans. Brigit Patmore* Macmillan, New York 1955
4   **SIR ALEXANDER CRICHTON, FRS (1763–1856) IMPERIAL RUSSIAN PHYSICIAN AT LARGE** *John H Appleby* Notes and Records of The Royal Society, London 1999
5   **UNPUBLISHED LETTER** *Edmund Butcher* Bristol Record Office
6   **YORK HERALD** June 21, 1826
7   **MORNING POST, LONDON** May 26, 1831
8   **MORNING POST, LONDON** June 2, 1831
9   **A HISTORY OF THE TOWN, PARISH AND MANOR OF SIDMOUTH VOL III** *Peter Orlando Hutchinson* 1880
10   **TREWMAN'S EXETER FLYING POST** June 30, 1831
11   **MORNING POST, LONDON** July 2, 1831
12   **HISTORIC SIDMOUTH: LIFE AND TIMES IN SIDMOUTH : A GUIDE TO THE BLUE PLAQUES** *Julia Creeke* Sid Vale Association 1992
13   **SIR ALEXANDER CRICHTON, FRS (1763–1856) IMPERIAL RUSSIAN PHYSICIAN AT LARGE** *John H Appleby* Notes and Records of The Royal Society, London 1999
14   **MORNING POST, LONDON** July 11, 1831
15   **MORNING POST, LONDON** August 11, 1831
16   **THE SIDMOUTH OBSERVER AND VISITORS' LIST** published by Arthur Caxton Day and Henry Burnell Day, High Street, Sidmouth September 28, 1982

CHAPTER 7 - ANOTHER FAMOUS RESIDENT

1   **SONNETS FROM THE PORTUGUESE LXIII** *Elizabeth Barrett Browning*
2   http://www.100greatblackbritons.com
3   **THE LETTERS OF ELIZABETH BARRETT BROWNING VOL I** *ed. Frederic G Kenyon* Macmillan, New York 1897
4   **LETTER 470 EBB TO LADY MARGARET COCKS** *Elizabeth Barrett Browning Society*
5   **THE LIFE OF ELIZABETH BARRETT BROWNING** *Gardner B Taplin* Yale University Press, New Haven CT 1957

6   cited in **WIKIPEDIA – Elizabeth Barrett Browning**
7   **THE LETTERS OF ELIZABETH BARRETT BROWNING VOL I** *ed. Frederic G Kenyon* Macmillan, New York 1897
8   **SIDMOUTH DEED OF 1836** *Original in Sidmouth Museum*
9   **THE RALEIGH COUNTRY** *Eric R Delderfield* Raleigh Press, Exmouth 1959
10   **SPEECH AT TAUNTON** *Sydney Smith* 1831

CHAPTER 8 – COLLECTING VICTORIANA
1   **LETHABY'S SIDMOUTH JOURNAL AND DIRECTORY** printed and published by Richard Lethaby, Market Place, Sidmouth March 1, 1864
2   **THE ENGLISH SEASIDE RESORT: A SOCIAL HISTORY 1750-1914** (p.222) *John K Walton* Leicester University Press 1983
3   **LETHABY'S SIDMOUTH JOURNAL AND DIRECTORY** printed and published by Richard Lethaby, Market Place, Sidmouth November 1, 1874
4   **ibid.** December 1, 1870
5   **SIDMOUTH CHRONICLES** *John Tindall* June 10, 1914

CHAPTER 9 – 1837 to 1849
1   **THE BEAUTIES OF THE SHORE** or A Guide To The Watering-Places On The South-East Coast Of Devon. (p.117) *D M Stirling* Exeter: printed for the author by W Roberts
2   **THE ENGLISH SEASIDE RESORT: A SOCIAL HISTORY 1750-1914** (p.19) *John K Walton* Leicester University Press 1983
3   **HISTORIC SIDMOUTH: LIFE AND TIMES IN SIDMOUTH : A GUIDE TO THE BLUE PLAQUES** *Julia Creeke* Sid Vale Association 1992
4   **A HISTORY OF THE TOWN, PARISH AND MANOR OF SIDMOUTH VOL III** *Peter Orlando Hutchinson* 1880
5   **THE ANNUAL REGISTER** *ed. Edmund Burke* 1844

CHAPTER 10 – 1850 to 1859
1   **THE BEAUTIES OF THE SHORE** or A Guide To The Watering-Places On The South-East Coast Of Devon. *D M Stirling* Exeter: printed for the author by W Roberts
2   **HARVEY'S SIDMOUTH DIRECTORY and general advertiser for Sidmouth and the neighbourhood** November 1, 1851
3   **ibid.** August 5, 1853
4   **A WATERBIOGRAPHY** *Robert C Leslie* Southampton: Ashford Press Publishing 1985
5   **ibid.** p109

CHAPTER 11 – 1860 to 1869
1   **LETHABY'S SIDMOUTH JOURNAL AND DIRECTORY** printed and published by Richard Lethaby, Market Place, Sidmouth May 1, 1862
2   **THE LEISURE HOUR** October 11, 1862 cited in **LETHABY'S SIDMOUTH JOURNAL** November 1, 1862
3   **LETHABY'S SIDMOUTH JOURNAL AND DIRECTORY** printed and published by Richard Lethaby, Market Place, Sidmouth June 1, 1864
4   **ibid.** July 1, 1865
5   **ibid.** July 1, 1866
6   **ibid.** January 1, 1867
7   **A STORY OF SIDMOUTH** (p.30) *Anna Sutton* James Townsend & Sons Ltd, Exeter 1959
8   **THE SIDMOUTH OBSERVER AND VISITORS' LIST** published by Arthur Caxton Day and Henry Burnell Day, High Street, Sidmouth July 27, 1892

CHAPTER 12 – 1870 to 1879
1   **LETHABY'S SIDMOUTH JOURNAL AND DIRECTORY** printed and published by Richard Lethaby, Market Place, Sidmouth August 1, 1870
2   **ibid.** December 1, 1870
3   **THE SIDMOUTH DIRECTORY AND GENERAL ADVERTISER** printed and published by Charles Culverwell, Fore Street, Sidmouth February 18, 1871

4   **LETHABY'S SIDMOUTH JOURNAL AND DIRECTORY** printed and published by Richard Lethaby, Market Place, Sidmouth   April 30, 1871

5   **THE SIDMOUTH DIRECTORY AND GENERAL ADVERTISER** printed and published by Charles Culverwell, Fore Street, Sidmouth   November 1, 1873

6   **LETHABY'S SIDMOUTH JOURNAL AND DIRECTORY** printed and published by Richard Lethaby, Market Place, Sidmouth   September 1, 1874

7   **ibid.**   August 1, 1878

8   **ibid.**   June 3, 1879

9   **A HISTORY OF THE PRESBYTERIAN AND GENERAL BAPTIST CHURCHES IN THE WEST OF ENGLAND WITH MEMOIRS OF SOME OF THE PASTORS**   *Jerom Murch*   London:R Hunter, 72 St Paul's Churchyard   1835

10   http://www.devon.gov.uk/localstudies/98965/1.html

11   **A HISTORY OF THE PRESBYTERIAN AND GENERAL BAPTIST CHURCHES IN THE WEST OF ENGLAND WITH MEMOIRS OF SOME OF THE PASTORS**   *Jerom Murch*   London:R Hunter, 72 St Paul's Churchyard   1835

12   **UNPUBLISHED LETTER** *Edmund Butcher* Bristol Records Office

13   **LETHABY'S SIDMOUTH JOURNAL AND DIRECTORY** printed and published by Richard Lethaby, Market Place, Sidmouth   August 1, 1872

CHAPTER 13 – 1880 to 1889

1   **LETHABY'S SIDMOUTH JOURNAL AND DIRECTORY** printed and published by Richard Lethaby, Market Place, Sidmouth   July 1, 1880

2   **VANITY FAIR** September 11, 1880 cited in **LETHABY'S SIDMOUTH JOURNAL AND DIRECTORY** October 1, 1880

3   **LETHABY'S SIDMOUTH JOURNAL AND DIRECTORY** printed and published by Richard Lethaby, Market Place, Sidmouth   February 1, 1884

4   **ibid.**   May 1, 1884

5   **THE SIDMOUTH DIRECTORY AND GENERAL ADVERTISER** printed and published by Charles Culverwell, Fore Street, Sidmouth   July 18, 1884

6   **LETHABY'S SIDMOUTH JOURNAL AND DIRECTORY** printed and published by Richard Lethaby, Market Place, Sidmouth   August 1, 1884

7   **THE SIDMOUTH DIRECTORY AND GENERAL ADVERTISER** printed and published by Charles Culverwell, Fore Street, Sidmouth   December 18, 1884

8   **LETHABY'S SIDMOUTH JOURNAL AND DIRECTORY** printed and published by Richard Lethaby, Market Place, Sidmouth   October 1, 1886

9   **ibid.**   December 1, 1886

10   **ibid.**   September 1, 1881

11   **THE SIDMOUTH DIRECTORY AND GENERAL ADVERTISER** printed and published by Charles Culverwell, Fore Street, Sidmouth   May 18, 1882

12   **ibid.**   January 3, 1883

13   **LETHABY'S SIDMOUTH JOURNAL AND DIRECTORY** printed and published by Richard Lethaby, Market Place, Sidmouth   June 19, 1884

14   **THE SIDMOUTH DIRECTORY AND GENERAL ADVERTISER** printed and published by Charles Culverwell, Fore Street, Sidmouth   June 25, 1887

15   **WILL OF MARY FLOYD 1782** Shropshire Record Office

16   **THE SIDMOUTH DIRECTORY AND GENERAL ADVERTISER** printed and published by Charles Culverwell, Fore Street, Sidmouth   June 3, 1881

17   **LETHABY'S SIDMOUTH JOURNAL AND DIRECTORY** printed and published by Richard Lethaby, Market Place, Sidmouth   July 1, 1881

18   **THE SIDMOUTH OBSERVER AND VISITORS' LIST** published by Arthur Caxton Day and Henry Burnell Day, High Street, Sidmouth   July 27, 1898

19   **ibid.**   August 3, 1898

CHAPTER 14 – 1890 to 1899

1   **THE SIDMOUTH OBSERVER AND VISITORS' LIST** published by Arthur Caxton Day and Henry Burnell Day, High Street, Sidmouth   January 7, 1891

2   **ibid.**   January 14, 1891

3   **ibid.**   January 28, 1891

4   **SAMPSON'S SIDMOUTH** *Sylvia Brownlee* Brownlee Publishing 2009
5   **THE SIDMOUTH OBSERVER AND VISITORS' LIST** published by Arthur Caxton Day
         and Henry Burnell Day, High Street, Sidmouth   July 20, 1892
6   **ibid.** July 27, 1892
7   **ibid.** August 24, 1892
8   **ibid.** February 8, 1893
9   **ibid.** June 13, 1894
10   **ibid.** September 27, 1893
11   **ibid.** March 24, 1894
12   **ibid.** July 17, 1895
13   **ibid.** July 31, 1895
14   **ibid.** April 10, 1895
15   **ibid.** March 3, 1897
16   **ibid.** June 23, 1897
17   **ibid.** October 6, 1897
18   **ibid.** August 25, 1897
19   **ibid.** June 8, 1898
20   **ibid.** June 16, 1897

CHAPTER 15 – 1900 to 1901
1   **THE SIDMOUTH OBSERVER AND VISITORS' LIST** published by Arthur Caxton Day

ABOUT THE AUTHOR

Dr Peter Fung was born in England. When he was three, his family moved to Trinidad in the West Indies, which was his father's homeland. He grew up and went to school there and in 1970 he returned to the UK, where he studied Marine Zoology at Bangor University and then Medicine at Southampton University. Having worked as a General Practitioner in Southampton for twenty years, and in Sidmouth for eight years, he retired in 2011.

Peter has had associations with the Sid Valley throughout his life, with relations living at various times in Sidford, Sidbury and Sidmouth. He remembers regular, but infrequent, childhood holidays in Sidford, and then longer spells while at University, during which he came to appreciate the special character of the Valley.

This connection was strengthened when he married a Sidmouth girl, whose family roots in Sidmouth go back several centuries. After a long and pleasant time in Southampton, with the family having left home, he and his wife returned to Sidmouth in 2003 and moved into Fortfield Terrace.

Like many Terrace residents of the past, he has enjoyed playing cricket, and still enjoys playing tennis at the Fort Field. Also like many former Terrace residents, he is a member of All Saints Church, where he is involved in leading worship.

also by this author:

ETERNITY NOW - Exploring the world of the eternal
A Christian view of eternity
Kingsway Publications 2001
ISBN 0-85476-921-8